Sacramental exercises. In two parts. ... By Jabez Earle, D.D. The eighth edition.

Jabez Earle

ECCO
PRINT EDITIONS

Gale ECCO Print Editions

Relive history with *Eighteenth Century Collections Online*, now available in print for the independent historian and collector. This series includes the most significant English-language and foreign-language works printed in Great Britain during the eighteenth century, and is organized in seven different subject areas including literature and language; medicine, science, and technology; and religion and philosophy. The collection also includes thousands of important works from the Americas.

The eighteenth century has been called "The Age of Enlightenment." It was a period of rapid advance in print culture and publishing, in world exploration, and in the rapid growth of science and technology – all of which had a profound impact on the political and cultural landscape. At the end of the century the American Revolution, French Revolution and Industrial Revolution, perhaps three of the most significant events in modern history, set in motion developments that eventually dominated world political, economic, and social life.

In a groundbreaking effort, Gale initiated a revolution of its own: digitization of epic proportions to preserve these invaluable works in the largest online archive of its kind. Contributions from major world libraries constitute over 175,000 original printed works. Scanned images of the actual pages, rather than transcriptions, recreate the works *as they first appeared.*

Now for the first time, these high-quality digital scans of original works are available via print-on-demand, making them readily accessible to libraries, students, independent scholars, and readers of all ages.

For our initial release we have created seven robust collections to form one the world's most comprehensive catalogs of 18th century works.

Initial Gale ECCO Print Editions collections include:

History and Geography
Rich in titles on English life and social history, this collection spans the world as it was known to eighteenth-century historians and explorers. Titles include a wealth of travel accounts and diaries, histories of nations from throughout the world, and maps and charts of a world that was still being discovered. Students of the War of American Independence will find fascinating accounts from the British side of conflict.

Social Science

Delve into what it was like to live during the eighteenth century by reading the first-hand accounts of everyday people, including city dwellers and farmers, businessmen and bankers, artisans and merchants, artists and their patrons, politicians and their constituents. Original texts make the American, French, and Industrial revolutions vividly contemporary.

Medicine, Science and Technology

Medical theory and practice of the 1700s developed rapidly, as is evidenced by the extensive collection, which includes descriptions of diseases, their conditions, and treatments. Books on science and technology, agriculture, military technology, natural philosophy, even cookbooks, are all contained here.

Literature and Language

Western literary study flows out of eighteenth-century works by Alexander Pope, Daniel Defoe, Henry Fielding, Frances Burney, Denis Diderot, Johann Gottfried Herder, Johann Wolfgang von Goethe, and others. Experience the birth of the modern novel, or compare the development of language using dictionaries and grammar discourses.

Religion and Philosophy

The Age of Enlightenment profoundly enriched religious and philosophical understanding and continues to influence present-day thinking. Works collected here include masterpieces by David Hume, Immanuel Kant, and Jean-Jacques Rousseau, as well as religious sermons and moral debates on the issues of the day, such as the slave trade. The Age of Reason saw conflict between Protestantism and Catholicism transformed into one between faith and logic -- a debate that continues in the twenty-first century.

Law and Reference

This collection reveals the history of English common law and Empire law in a vastly changing world of British expansion. Dominating the legal field is the *Commentaries of the Law of England* by Sir William Blackstone, which first appeared in 1765. Reference works such as almanacs and catalogues continue to educate us by revealing the day-to-day workings of society.

Fine Arts

The eighteenth-century fascination with Greek and Roman antiquity followed the systematic excavation of the ruins at Pompeii and Herculaneum in southern Italy; and after 1750 a neoclassical style dominated all artistic fields. The titles here trace developments in mostly English-language works on painting, sculpture, architecture, music, theater, and other disciplines. Instructional works on musical instruments, catalogs of art objects, comic operas, and more are also included.

The BiblioLife Network

This project was made possible in part by the BiblioLife Network (BLN), a project aimed at addressing some of the huge challenges facing book preservationists around the world. The BLN includes libraries, library networks, archives, subject matter experts, online communities and library service providers. We believe every book ever published should be available as a high-quality print reproduction; printed on-demand anywhere in the world. This insures the ongoing accessibility of the content and helps generate sustainable revenue for the libraries and organizations that work to preserve these important materials.

The following book is in the "public domain" and represents an authentic reproduction of the text as printed by the original publisher. While we have attempted to accurately maintain the integrity of the original work, there are sometimes problems with the original work or the micro-film from which the books were digitized. This can result in minor errors in reproduction. Possible imperfections include missing and blurred pages, poor pictures, markings and other reproduction issues beyond our control. Because this work is culturally important, we have made it available as part of our commitment to protecting, preserving, and promoting the world's literature.

GUIDE TO FOLD-OUTS MAPS and OVERSIZED IMAGES

The book you are reading was digitized from microfilm captured over the past thirty to forty years. Years after the creation of the original microfilm, the book was converted to digital files and made available in an online database.

In an online database, page images do not need to conform to the size restrictions found in a printed book. When converting these images back into a printed bound book, the page sizes are standardized in ways that maintain the detail of the original. For large images, such as fold-out maps, the original page image is split into two or more pages

Guidelines used to determine how to split the page image follows:

• Some images are split vertically; large images require vertical and horizontal splits.
• For horizontal splits, the content is split left to right.
• For vertical splits, the content is split from top to bottom.
• For both vertical and horizontal splits, the image is processed from top left to bottom right.

SACRAMENTAL EXERCISES.

IN TWO PARTS.

FIRST,

The CHRISTIAN's Employment

BEFORE, AT, and AFTER

The LORD's SUPPER.

SECOND,

The CHRISTIAN's CONDUCT in
his AFTER-LIFE.

By JABEZ EARLE, D.D.

The EIGHTH EDITION.

LONDON:

Printed for J. BUCKLAND, in Pater-noster Row,

M,DCC,LXXIV,

TO THE

R E A D E R.

IT is sad to consider, how many professed christians *live in the* utter neglect *of the* Lord's Supper; *and how few* communicants *are careful to prepare* duly, *eat and drink* worthily, *and live* answerably.

A great deal has been written upon this occasion: *to which I have added the following* sheets; *which I may be allowed, I hope, to publish, without being thought to pretend to any thing* extraordinary, *or* detract *from the* excellent performances *of others.*

For, while the case requires and admits help, *there can be no harm in making further trials; especially in those circumstances, where the most* likely means *are not ever the most* effectual. *But success*

more

more especially depends upon the divine *blessing, which is not always given in regular proportion to the natural aptitude of the means; but sometimes in a sovereign and unaccountable manner,* that no flesh should glory in his presence.

However, it is too plain to be denied: that the different capacities *and* relishes *of men make a variety useful, if not necessary; and that there may be a concurrence of many* other circumstances, *which shall give a* meaner *performance the advantage with some people as to usefulness, above others that are* more sprightly *and* elaborate. *Nay, it is no impossible thing, that a man may read a book upon some* foreign consideration; *which shall be blessed to do him that good, which could never be expected from better discourses* not known of, *or* not minded.

Upon these accounts I have published the ensuing papers; *hoping they may be useful to* some, *whatever their* general entertainment be.

THE
CONTENTS.

PART I.

CHAP. I. *THE* christian *convinced, that it is his* duty *to come to the* Lord's Table. Page 7

CHAP. II. *The* christian *resolved to offer himself to* communion. 11

CHAP. III. *After having been approved by the* minister, *and allowed to* communicate. 14

CHAP. IV. *The* christian *preparing for the* Lord's Supper. 19

CHAP. V. *The* christian *at the* Lord's Table. 51

CHAP. VI. *The* christian *in his retirements, after the* Lord's Supper. 59

A 3

CONTENTS.

PART II.

CHAP. I. *Of reviewing our behaviour* at *the ordinance.* 83

CHAP. II. *Shewing our* duty, *if upon examination we find our* attendance *has been in the main* regular. 88

CHAP. III. *Shewing our* duty, *if our* attendance *has been very* irregular, *or* uncomfortable. 104

CHAP. IV. *Recommending the frequent* recollection *of what passed at the* sacrament, *in order to our* spiritual improvement. 109

CHAP. V. *Representing the* advantages, *which will arise from this practice; particularly in reference to* succeeding *opportunities.* 121

APPENDIX.

I. *A prayer for a* particular *person,* before *receiving the sacrament of the* Lord's Supper.

II. *A prayer,* after *receiving the* Lord's Supper.

PART I.

THE

Chriſtian's Employment

Before, at, and after the

LORD's SUPPER.

CHAP. I.

The Chriſtian *convinced, that it is his* Duty *to come to the* Lord's Table.

DO *this in remembrance of me* [1 Cor. xi. 25.] It is the voice of my Lord; and left I ſhould think it was directed only to his twelve diſciples, or the *chriſtians* of the firſt ages, St. *Paul* aſſures me, that this ordinance is to run parallel with time, and by it the church is to *ſhow forth* Chriſt's *death 'till he come.* Conſider, O my ſoul! Is the *Lord at hand?,* will he *ſurely come quickly?* how ſhall I anſwer it in that day, that I have neglected ſo expreſs a command ſ

A 4   a coma command not couched in ambiguous and uncertain terms, but delivered in as plain and positive expressions, as any in the Bible. *Sure I am more brutish than any man, and have not the understanding of a man!* I have professed a mighty respect to the authority of my Redeemer, and a vast reverence for his laws; but how unaccountably have I managed! as though I were to chuse, what commands I would please to obey; and were vested with a dispensing power, superior to the obligation of *his* precepts, to whom *all power is given both in heaven and in earth.* [Matt. xxviii. 18.]

Blush, O my soul, and be ashamed at so inconsistent a conduct! either Christ is thy prince and law-giver, or he is not. *If not,* profess thyself an infidel, and renounce thy baptism. *If he be,* obey him in all that he requires: and either believe that he has not made it thy duty to remember him; or yield a chearful subjection in *this,* as well as *other* instances.

When he has said, *do this;* either he does not mean what he says, or does not speak to thee: or else thy disobedience is at once inexcusable and unaccountable.

Can the words be wrested? is any *sophistry* capable of contesting their sense? what can *do this,* signify less than a positive command? or, how can the will of my prince be ever signified, so as to oblige me, if so plain terms are by any cavil to be eluded?

But

But does he speak to me? if I were a true disciple, I were indeed within the compass of the law; and must be either a *communicant* or a *rebel*.

Consider, O my soul! and don't rashly dash thy hopes, to escape thy duty. 'Tis true, I am not such a christian as I should be: but am I willing to have my name missing in the book of life? can I be content to resign my birth-right, and own that I have *neither lot nor portion* in the Son of GOD? would I be passed by, when the *Lord shall count and write up the people?* [Psal. lxxxvii. 6.] Either I am a christian, or I am not: if I am, *this commandment is for me:* if I am not, what am I? a child of wrath, and a subject of the devil: and is such a condition tolerable? let me give up myself to Christ immediately: make no tarrying, O my soul, lest the avenger of blood overtake thee, and lest, if thou trifle *to-day*, thou be lost *to-morrow*. If I have been but *almost persuaded to be a christian* hitherto; it is high time that I make an absolute, unreserved surrender of myself to Christ presently, without any farther delay: and then let what I have done here *in secret*, be publickly owned and avouched at the *Lord's table*.

' And now, Lord, *all my desire is before*
' *thee*: I am convinced of my duty, and
' dare no longer disobey. Oh! forgive
' me,

' me, that I have rebelled so long ! I have
' been *invited* to thy table, and foolishly neg-
' lected many an opportunity of strengthen-
' ing and refreshing my soul.   I have been
' *commanded* to attend in remembrance of
' *him*, who deserves never to be forgotten ;
' and by my neglect have at once poured
' contempt upon *thy* authority, and slighted
' *his* love, who *loved me, and gave himself*
' *for me*.

  ' I bless thee, that I am in some mea-
' sure sensible of my error ; and am come to
' a resolution, that I will have respect to *this*,
' as well as *other* commands.   The time past
' shall suffice me to have lived in the omis-
' sion of so plain a *duty*, and the neglect
' of so glorious a *privilege* · oh ! *keep it upon*
' *the imagination of my heart for ever* ; and
' let me be confirmed in those good pur-
' poses, which thy own spirit has led me to
' form, and no less power than his can help
' me to keep.

  ' I am indeed *unworthy* ; but acknow-
' ledge the insufficiency of that plea, against
' a *positive* command.   I am unworthy, but
' must not therefore refuse thy kindness, I
' hope I am in Christ, though the meanest
' soul that relates to him, and therefore can-
' not any longer want an ordinance ; in the
' use of which, I hope *to grow in grace, and*
' *in the knowledge of my Lord*.

' Or,

' Or, if I have hitherto deceived myself,
' and *walked in a vain shew*, I now desire to
' accept of the gospel-offer, to own my bap-
' tismal covenant, to avouch thee, O Fa-
' ther, Son, and Spirit, to be my God, my
' all, my everlasting portion. Upon my
' bended knees I now accept an offered Sa-
' viour, and call heaven and earth to witness,
' that, as far as I can judge, I am sincere.
' And this I would declare in the presence
' of thy people; begging with some hope
' and confidence, that I may be accepted
' *now*, and found in the number of the faith-
' ful *at last*.

' O direct me in all the steps I am to take;
' and let me see my way, and follow it, and
' have comfort in the issue, through the me-
' rits and mediation of my Lord and Saviour
' Jesus Christ.' *Amen.*

CHAP. II.

The Christian *resolved to offer himself to the* Communion.

NOW, O my soul, thou hast *opened thy mouth to the Lord, and canst not go back!* Thy next duty is to apply thyself to the *minister*, who is the *steward of these myste-ries*; [1 Cor. iv. 1.] that, if he judge thee

meet,

meet, he may *admit* thee to the holy *solemnity*. Let me not be foolifhly *bafhful*, much lefs act the *hypocrite*; but ufe the utmoft franknefs with my fpiritual guide: that he may be able to pafs the better judgment upon my cafe, let me ftate it *fairly*; neither pretend to what I have not received, nor deny what I have. *This* would be bafe ingratitude; *that* impious mockery. If thou haft a prudent, faithful minifter to apply thyfelf to; freely open thy breaft, and unbofom thy foul: tell him thy defires, and their motives; confefs thy fears, doubts, and jealoufies; beg his prayers; and reverence his judgment. If he fhould think thee *unfit*, be not provoked nor difcouraged; but take his counfel, and wait with patience till he judge thee fufficiently inftructed and duly qualified. If he exprefs his *satisfaction*, don't diftruft him; but believe him a more capable judge of thy cafe, than thou art thyfelf. Not that thou fhouldft efteem him *infallible*; 'tis his *mafter*'s province to fearch hearts: but fure *his* judgment deferves the fame regard, as a *phyfician*'s about thy body, or a *lawyer*'s concerning thy eftate. Be faithful in the account of thyfelf, and doubt not, but he'll be faithful in delivering his opinion. And with his faithfulnefs thou mayeft expect tendernefs, condefcenfion and compaffion, in imitation of the *chief Shepherd*, who is *meek and lowly in heart*.

heart; [Matt. xi. 29.] *who will not quench the smoaking flax, nor break the bruised reed.* [Matt. xii. 20.]

‘ Oh that God, who has convinced me of
‘ my duty, and brought me to a refolution,
‘ would help me to be open and fincere!
‘ Let me not go about to impofe upon thy
‘ minifter; which would be juftly interpreted
‘ as an attempt to impofe upon my Lord
‘ himfelf, *whofe eyes are as a flame of fire*;
‘ who can't be *deceived*, as *knowing what is
‘ in man*; and will not be *mocked*, as being a
‘ *jealous God*. O give me *freedom*, that I
‘ may utter what I have felt, give me *humi-
‘ lity*, that I may not be afhamed to difcover
‘ thofe follies and imperfections, that may be
‘ at the bottom of my doubts and fcruples:
‘ give me a *teachable difpofition*, that I may
‘ not defpife inftruction: help me to remem-
‘ ber the relation, in which thefe under fhep-
‘ herds ftand to the *great fhepherd and bifhop of
‘ fouls.* [1 Pet. ii. 25.]

‘ Let me not *defpife* his judgment of my
‘ cafe, nor yet lay *too great a ftrefs* upon it;
‘ remembering that minifters may accept,
‘ where GOD may reject; and admit thofe to
‘ the facrament, as qualified for communion
‘ with the church, who yet fhall be found
‘ unworthy receivers, as not having a *wedding
‘ garment*.

‘ Oh direct thy fervant, that he may
‘ deal *prudently* and *tenderly*, and yet withal
‘ *faith-*

' *faithfully.* Let him be duly apprized of my
' cafe, and pass such a verdict as the great
' judge will ratify.'

CHAP. III.

After having been approved by the Mini-
ster, and allowed to communicate.

BE thankful, O my soul, that GOD has
heard the voice of thy supplication!
His *minister* has dealt tenderly and faithfully
with thee, has encouraged thy design, promised thee the assistance of his prayers, given
thee instruction, and suitable advice; and
nothing more remains, but thy *actual prepa-*
ration for that holy ordinance.

But, O see to it, that thy heart be *right.*
'Tis a *deceitful* heart thou haft to manage:
look to thyself, that thy *goodness* be not *as*
the morning cloud, and *early dew, that soon*
passeth away. Remember the warning the
minister gave thee, that thou shouldest not
act in such a case without serious thought,
and mature deliberation, left *rash* engagements should issue in *broken* vows, and *cursed*
apostacy.

Take heed, O my soul, that I be not
another instance, to confirm the truth of
that awful observation; (of which he *told*
me weeping) that many *hot* professors have
dwindled

dwindled into *luke-warm* chriftians, and fome-times fell headlong into the *gulf* of profanenefs. and infidelity. Tremble to think, if this fhould be thy fad cafe; and let thy fear quicken thy application, that thou mayft not *end in the flefh*, after having *begun in the fpirit*.

Yet let me not be difcouraged. 'Tis indeed a great thing to be a chriftian : but great is the grace and mercy of GOD; great is the merit, and prevalent the interceffion of my Redeemer, who has prayed for his difciples, that their *faith fail* not; [Luke xxii. 32.] great is the power of the Holy Ghoft, who can preferve my graces, fubdue my corruptions, help me to crucify the world, and refift and vanquifh the devil. Never forget the encouragement he gave me to hope, that if my heart don't reproach me, as acting deceitfully in my profeffions and engagements ; and if I will keep clofe to GOD in the way of his appointments, I need not fear being accepted of him now, and having the good work begun, *carried on to the day of Jefus.*

But, O my foul, fee to it ; and again, I fay, fee to it, that thou do *with full purpofe of heart cleave to the Lord :* that thy prefent devotion don't prove a fudden flafh ; but having fet *thy hand to the plough,* don't think *of looking back.* Remember that awful text,

It

It had been better for them, not to have known the way of righteousness, than, after they have known it, to turn from the holy commandment. [2 Pet. ii. 21.] Let this word be a spur to thy diligence; but not revive thy scruples. It were better never to communicate, than afterwards to apostatize.

But, will this be a plea for thy disobedience?—Consider, O my soul, at this rate, thou shouldst never have been baptized; never called thyself a christian; never joined thyself to a worshipping assembly; never heard a sermon, or put up a prayer; never given an alms, or performed a duty of any sort; seeing all these will aggravate thy misery, if thou provest a hypociite or apostate at last.

Therefore, in the strength of Christ, hold on thy way: don't decline thy *Lord's table*, but prepare for it; that, being a worthy communicant here, thou mayst at last be a *partaker of the inheritance of the saints in light.*

Attempt all this in a better strength than thy own; ever remembering, that of thyself thou canst do nothing; and that God's grace is at once necessary and sufficient for thee.

‘ Now, O my God, I adore and praise
‘ thee, that I have been enabled to open
‘ my case to thy minister; and that thou
‘ hast inclined his heart kindly to *encourage*
‘ me, wisely to *instruct* me, and faithfully

3

‘ ℧

' to *warn* me ; 'O may thy good fpirit make
' his endeavours effectual, that I may re-
' ceive inftruction and take warning. I am,
' fenfible of the treachery and bafenefs of
' my own heart, but I am alfo acquainted
' with thy power, and mercy, and faithful-
' nefs. Oh! let me not rafhly take up a
' profeffion, which I fhall as haftily abandon,
' or never live up to.

' Help me to underftand the engage-
' ments I am going under, that I may
' count the coft, and not prove a foolifh
' builder : help me to confider the difficulties
' and difadvantages that attend religion, and
' the troubles it may expofe me to : may I
' ferioufly confider, that I muft *deny myfelf*,
' and *take up my crofs*, and *follow Chrift*, if I
' would be *his difciple*.

' Yet let none of thefe things *move* me
' from my refolution. O give me fuch near
' and affecting views of *the glory that is to*
' *be revealed*, and of that *wrath and fiery*
' *indignation* which awaits the ungodly : *fo*
' fet death and judgment before me, as to
' imprefs me with a fenfe of the worth of
' my foul, and the emptinefs of this world ;
' that I may be fully determined to accept of
' Chrift, and adhere to him with all his dif-
' advantages ; that I may *count all things*
' *but lofs, for the excellency of the knowledge*
' *of him !* [Philip. iii. 8.] And O may this
' be my unalterable perfuafion ! Let me ne-

' ver

' ver turn aſide, nor go a-whoring from
' thee. Oh! let me not wander from thy
' commandments! let me never, like an
' ungracious prodigal, forſake my father's
' houſe, or count his *meat contemptible.* O
' never let me deny or forget that Jeſus,
' who I am ſo ſolemnly to remember and
' avouch for my Lord and my God. Let
' the unclean devil never re-enter, and take
' poſſeſſion of this ſoul, which I conſecrate
' as a *temple to the Holy Ghoſt.* I am full of
' fears, and have reaſon to be jealous of
' myſelf, but yet I am not void of hope;
' nor have I any reaſon to diſtruſt my God :
' thy grace is ſufficient for me, O for *thy*
' *name's ſake, lead me and guide me ; put thy*
' *fear into my heart; that I may never depart*
' *from thee.*

' Lord, let not the deceitfulneſs of my
' own heart, the incumbrances of the wo ld,
' or the ſolicitations of the devil, put me by
' the deſign I have formed of attending at
' thy table: may a ſenſe of duty outweigh
' a thouſand excuſes; and hopes of gracious
' aſſiſtance, and merciful acceptance, ſilence
' all my fears.

' Yet let me not come *unworthily!* may
' I never *eat and drink judgment to myſelf?*
' Deliver me from the dreadful guilt of *cru-*
' *cifying afreſh, and putting to open ſhame*
' that Jeſus, whom I think my ſoul loves,
' and I deſire to remember, avouch and ho-
' nour :-

' nour : keep me from the great unhappine∫s
' of being poisoned by the riche∫t food, and
' highe∫t cordial ; of coming for *a ble∫∫ing*,
' and carrying away *a cur∫e*. *Amen*, for Je∫us
' ∫ake.'

CHAP. IV.

The Chri∫tian *preparing for the* Lord's
Supper.

SECT. I.

COn∫ider, O my ∫oul, the day is near, in
which I am to appear at the table of
my Lord ! it concerns me to *prepare*, that I
may be a *welcome* gue∫t, and a *worthy* receiver.
To prepare ! tho' the expre∫∫ion be ∫hort, 'tis
comprehen∫ive ; and I ∫hall find it implies
more work, than can be crouded into a little
time, or done with a little pains. Let me
therefore redeem ∫ome time from my bu∫ine∫s,
at lea∫t from my plea∫ures, before the week
be far advanced ; that unfore∫een occurrences
may not deprive me of an opportunity to dre∫s
my ∫oul for the glorious ∫olemnity, and put
me upon the unhappy plunge of mi∫∫ing the
fea∫t, or wanting the *wedding garment*.

And, O my ∫oul, exert thy∫elf, let all thy
powers be upon the ∫tretch. *What, thou finde∫t
to do, do it with all thy might ;* that thou
mayst

mayſt not ridiculouſly trifle away that time which thou ſeemeſt conſcientiouſly to redeem.

See to it, that in thy retirements thou be *really* alone; that the world don't follow thee into thy cloſet; nor thy thoughts fly abroad into the world, and leave a heartleſs carcaſs to entertain thy GOD. If thy mind be not fixed upon the work before thee, thy retirements will be but ſolemn idleneſs: or if the world be admitted to put thee by thy duty, the cloſet will be but a more private *compting-houſe.*

S E C T. II.

LET me now, O my ſoul, prepare for my preparations. Let me lay down the plan of my deſign, that I may not be at a loſs how to manage; but may go regularly on, without that confuſion of thought, which will leſſen the pleaſure and profit of my work.

There appear to be ſeveral *branches* of that buſineſs, which is called by the *general* name of *preparation.* But before I enter upon particulars, I would firſt be deeply poſſeſſed of the *neceſſity* of the duty in general; which will quicken me to the greater care and ſeriouſneſs in a buſineſs that ſo well deſerves it.

To this end conſider cloſely, that an *unprepared* communicant muſt neceſſarily be

an *unworthy* one.   And the danger of eating
and drinking unworthily is reprefented by
St. *Paul* in very awful terms; fuch a one *eats
and drinks damnation to himfelf.*

Damnation! Tremble, O my foul, at the
difmal thought! fure it fhould ftrike a chil-
nefs into my blood, and a horror into my
fpirit! can any tongue exprefs, can any mind
conceive the direful contents of that expreffion? However interpreters may *foften* it, the
threatening can never be *difarmed* · the thunder
of it muft needs put a tender fpirit into con-
vulfions and agonies, at leaft affect him to a
very high degree.

To *eat and drink judgment to one's felf*, can
fignify no lefs than falling under the difpleafure of the living GOD. and who knows,
what it is to be the object of *his* angry refentments, in whofe *favour is life*, and whofe
wrath is worfe than death? If I eat and
drink unworthily, the leaft I can expect is
temporal ftrokes; I am in danger of *fpiritual* ones, and deferve *eternal* vengeance.
Indeed there is forgivenefs with God; but
fhall I fin, becaufe grace abounds? at that
rate, I may venture in defiance of that word,
whoremongers and adulterers God will judge,
&c. or commit the worft of villanies, becaufe GOD is *good and plenteous in mercy.*

Nor yet fhall this thought deter me from
my duty; for upon the fame principle I muft
abftain from · hearing, becaufe that will
aggravate

aggravate my condemnation, if I am found disobedient *The prayer of the wicked is an abomination* ; yea, *the ploughing of the wicked is sin* . and shall I therefore forsake the public worship of God, or neglect the business of my particular calling ?

But, O my soul, let this thought affect thee, so as to quicken thy endeavours, that thou mayst be admitted to the *Lord's table*, as a worthy receiver, and return *rejoicing in the God of thy salvation* : let the hopes of this put life into thy attempts : think, and think again, how vast will be the advantage of worthy receiving ! what words can express the blessed consequences of a regular attendance at the *Lord's table* ?

I may expect to have my *faith* strengthned by the representation of my Lord's sufferings : I may hope to have my *love* to him inflamed by the remembrance of his expensive *love* to me ; my *resolutions* confirmed ; my *mind* more spiritualized ; and my *whole conversation* made more regular. I may meet with sweet *peace*, and strong *consolation* ; yea, perhaps with rapturous *joy, joy unspeakable and full of glory*: [1 Pet. i. 8.] something that shall prove a cordial under the future *troubles of life*, and in the *agonies* of *death* too. I may there meet with *him* whom my soul loves ; and have such tokens of his love, as shall in the remembrance prove a *continual feast*.

But

But however, If I am sincere, I shall not be wholly disappointed: *my labour shall not be in vain in the Lord*. I shall get *real* good, if not *sensible*; if not *present*, yet *certain*. I shall reap what I sow, though it be long first. The harvest will be *sure*, though *late*, and then I shall have an abundant recompence for all the fatigue of the seed-time.

Come then, O my soul, up and be doing; spare no pains in a matter that deserves the utmost diligence, and will well reward it. And that thou mayst not do this important work negligently, lift up thy heart to the father of spirits; without whose gracious influences thou canst do nothing.

' O my GOD, *the preparation of the heart*
' *of man* is from thee. This I desire to be
' so sensible of, as to beg with the utmost
' earnestness, that I may be enabled to pre-
' pare myself suitably to so solemn an *or-*
' *dinance*

' Oh! impress me with an awful sense of
' the danger of receiving unworthily, that
' I may not dare to trifle with thee, the
' holy and jealous GOD: make me duly to
' consider the inexpressible advantage of
' worthy receiving; that I may not at once
' sin against thee, and wrong my own soul,
' by a negligent behaviour: direct me in
' every step I am to take, enlighten my mind,
' enlarge my heart, raise my affections, keep
' off the tempter, keep down my corrup-

' tions;

' tions; and so help me in the whole of my
' duty, that I may have this token for good,
' that thou designest to meet me and bless me
' at that holy solemnity ! It is a great thing to
' be duly prepared; but *thy grace is sufficient*
' *for me*; *let thy strength be made perfect in my*
' *weakness*, and the praise shall be thine own.'

SECT. III.

LET *a man examine himself, and so let him eat*, says the inspired apostle. Come then, O my soul, call thyself to an account, whether thou *art* in any measure that, which GOD expects every worthy communicant *should be*.

Have I *knowledge to discern the Lord's body?* am I apprized of the nature and end of this ordinance? has not the minister *bestowed upon me labour in vain*, when he opened these mysteries to me? has what I have read and heard about this matter, given me a tolerable notion of it? I know, a man may have knowledge enough, and yet eat and drink unworthily; but yet, without some good measure of understanding, he cannot be an *acceptable* communicant.

Do I therefore understand the nature of the gospel-covenant, the covenant of grace, of which the *sacraments* are *seals?*

Do I know how the *first* covenant was broken? into what a sad condition the fall
of

of our firft parents brought their wretched offspring? how it ple fe.l God in infinite mercy to enter into a *new* covenant, through a Redeemer, in which he has provided for *his own* honour and *our* happinefs? do I underftand who is the *mediator*, what the *bleffings*, and what the *terms* of this covenant?

Do I underftand the *relation* that this *facrament* bears to that *covenant*? that it is *inftituted* by the mediator, to whom *all power is given, both in heaven and earth*? [Matt xxviii. 18.] that it is defigned to reprefent the bleffings he has purchafed, with the manner in which they were procured, and are applied? that I am at the Lord's table to *fhew forth his death*? that the broken *bread* reprefents his *body*, which was broken for us; and the *wine* his precious *blood* which was fhed for us? our *eating* that bread, and *drinking* that cup, fignifies that fiducial feeding upon him, who is that (and more) to our *fouls*, that bread, the *ftaff of life*, and *wine* that *chears the heart*, is to our *bodies*.

Do I underftand how it *feals* the covenant to every worthy receiver? how hereby God obliges himfelf to be their God, to pardon their fins, fanctify their fouls, and at laft bring them to eternal happinefs and glory? how herein they engage themfelves to him, thankfully accepting what he offers, and chearfully complying with what he de-

B   mands?

mands? that herein we open our mouths to GoD, and fwear, that we will be his, in the bonds of an *everlafting covenant, that fhall not be forgotten,* accepting *him,* and refigning *ourfelves*

Do I know of what *advantage* this ordinance is to every worthy communicant? how it is defigned to confirm their faith, to enflame their love, purify their confciences, and comfort their fouls?

Do I underftand how it *produces* thefe effects? Not in a *natural* way, nor *merely* in a *moral* one; but by the powerful influences of the *fpirit,* difpenfed, and to be expected in a devout attendance upon the appointments of infinite wifdom and goodnefs. Let me put to my own foul that queftion, which my Saviour put to his difciples, *haft thou underftood all thefe things?*

I muft confefs my apprehenfions of thefe things are too dark and confufed; but I dare not deny the grace of GoD, who has given me fome acquaintance with thefe awful myfteries: and I hope I do defire to improve in knowledge, and am willing to receive inftruction.

' And O that GoD would teach me what
' I yet know not, and lead me farther into
' the knowlege of all neceffary truth! Oh
' that he would *fhew me his covenant* ; [Pfal.
' xxv. 14.] and help me to *grow in grace,*
' *and in the knowledge of my Lord and Saviour*
' *Jefus*

' *Jesus Christ!* [2 Pet. iii. 18.] that he would
' reveal to me by his spirit those *deep things*
' *of* God, which the *natural man receiveth*
' *not, because they are spiritually discerned?*
' [1 Cor. ii. 14.] O *father of lights, who*
' *givest wisdom liberally and upbraidest not,*
' *make me to know the love of Christ, which*
' *passeth knowledge, and help me to compre-*
' *hend, with all saints, the breadth, and length,*
' *and depth, and heighth of it.* [Eph. iii. 18,
' 19.] Amen.'

S E C T. IV.

COnsider, O my soul, that mere knowledge is not a *sufficient* qualification
for the holy communion. If I have *knowledge* to discern the Lord's body, and want
faith to feed upon him; I shall return from
his table disappointed and ashamed My
blessed Lord has told me, that, *except I eat
his flesh, and drink his blood, I have no life in
me.* [John vi. 53.] Now this I know must be
by *faith,* not after a corporal and carnal manner: let me therefore put that question to my
soul, which my Saviour put to his disciples;
where is thy faith? do I believe in an unseen
Jesus? do I heartily approve the method
which God has appointed for man's salvation,
that *being justified by faith,* he should *have
peace with God through our Lord Jesus Christ?*
do I heartily *submit to the righteousness of God?*

and

and *rejoice in God through* him, *by whom we have now received the atonement?* do I earneſtly deſire to *be found in Chriſt, not having mine own righteouſneſs,* &c. *but that which is through the faith of Chriſt, the righteouſneſs which is of God by faith,* that Chriſt may be *made* unto me *righteouſneſs?* believing *this* as a *principal* article of my religion, that *Chriſt died for our ſins,* and ſo was *made ſin* (a ſin-offering) *for us, that we might be made the righteouſneſs of God in him?* and do I accordingly lay the ſtreſs of my hopes upon the mercy of GOD in Chriſt, and under a conſciouſneſs of guilt apply to that *blood, which cleanſes from all ſin?* can my ſoul make her applications to him, and derive from *his fulneſs, even grace for grace?* am I in any meaſure acquainted with this myſtery? and can I underſtand, by any experience of my own, what the apoſtle meant when he ſaid, *I live; yet not I, but Chriſt liveth in me?* [Gal. ii. 20] What ſhould he do at a royal feaſt, that cannot taſte of the proviſion? am I therefore taught of GOD to believe in Jeſus?

' *Lord, I believe, help thou my unbelief!* I
' hope I have *taſted that the Lord is gracious.*
' I can remember, when I have ſat under
' his *ſhadow with great delight,* and *his fruit*
' *has been ſweet unto my taſte. My ſoul has*
' *followed hard after him,* and I have reaſon to
' *remember his love more than wine.*—But alas!

I

' I have

' I have too much occasion for that prayer,
' *Lord, increase my faith!* without controversy,
' *great is the mystery of godliness*; and I am
' too often apt to stumble at the cross: my
' temptations to unbelief often find me much
' forrowful employment, and at best my
' faith is but weak and languid. O my GOD,
' *perfect that which is lacking in my faith*; and
' when I find its *strength*, I shall not doubt its
' *reality.*'

SECT. V.

I Must also enquire concerning my *repentance.* An *impenitent* communicant I
know must be an *unworthy* one. That I
am a *sinner*, is a matter past question, and
that *as such* I am exposed to the displeasure of
GOD; so that, if he should enter into judgment with me, I could not stand, is what I
know and believe: yea, that the *least* sin I
ever committed *deserves* the wrath and curse
of GOD, both in this world, and that which
is to come. But all this is general and common, let me therefore, O my soul, press the
matter close and home. And,

First, Have I *laid* these things to *heart*?
have my convictions been affecting? have I
not only *known*, but *felt* these things? have
I been *weary and heavy laden* under a sense of
sin? have I groaned and trembled under
the apprehension of GOD's displeasure? has

B 3 *destruction*

deſtruction from the Lord been a terror to me? has *my fleſh trembled for fear of him, and have I been afraid of his judgments?* yea, have I been aſhamed of ſin, as a nauſeous, loathſome, filthy thing; contrary to the nature and law of God, and my own happineſs too; which conſiſts in conformity to God, and enjoyment of him? has the remembrance of my ſin filled my heart with grief, and my face with ſhame? eſpecially conſidering how it has been committed againſt a God of infinite *love* and *goodneſs?* does *this thought* give a peculiar accent to my grief, that I have ſinned againſt a *bleeding, dying* Jeſus, and a *forbearing* and *forgiving* God? and does the apprehenſion of pardoning mercy, through a redeemer, promote in me the moſt kindly relentings? according to that, *Ezek.* xvi. 63.

In the next place, have I been *influenced* by theſe convictions to take up a hearty and ſincere *resolution* of better obedience? do I hate *every falſe way?* and have I a *reſpect to all God's commandments?* Oh! let me remember, that nothing is repentance that conſiſts with an *habitual* love to any ſin, or an *allowed* averſion to any inſtance of duty, or branch of holineſs: is my *heart* and *life* changed? he that is the ſame *after* repentance as he was *before*, can never be accounted a true penitent.

O my

O my confcience, be faithful · have I *put off the old man with his lufts, and put on the new man, which after God is created in righteoufnefs and true holinefs?*

I hope it is thus with me, in fome meafure, that, though I offend in *many things*, I allow myfelf in *nothing*, that GOD in his word difallows.——But alas ! my repentance is far fhort of what I know *it fhould be*, and wifh it *were*.

' Oh ! that he, *whofe gift* repentance (as
' well as faith) is, would carry on the work
' which, I truft, is begun ! Lord, open
' my eyes, that I may fee more of the evil
' of fin : ftrike this heart, this rock, that it
' may more freely bleed at the remembrance
' of my paft follies : confirm my refolutions,
' that I may have *nothing more to do with idols*,
' but may be *ftedfaft and unmoveable, and al-*
' *ways abounding in the work of the Lord. fearch*
' *me and try me, and fee if there be any wicked*
' *way in me, and lead me in the way everlafting.*'

S E C T.   VI.

I Muft alfo examine myfelf concerning my *love*, an effential and comprehenfive grace. If I don't fincerely love the mafter of the bleffed feaft, and all the *regular* guefts, I can't be welcome. Come then, O my foul, is thy *heart circumcifed to love the Lord thy God with all thy heart, and*

B 4. *with*

with all thy foul? [Deut. xxx. 6] *this is the firft and great commandment.* canft thou truly fay, that thy *defire* is towards him, and thy *delight* in him? doft thou love *not in word and in tongue, but in deed and in truth?* [1 John iii. 18.] has he the pre-eminence in thy foul? canft thou fay, *whom have I in heaven* but thee, *and* there is *none upon earth* that *I can defire befides thee?* [Pfal. lxxiii 25] is Chrift precious to thee beyond comparifon and competition? and canft thou truly fay; *yea, doubtlefs, I count all things but lofs, for the excellency of the knowledge of Chrift Jefus my Lord?* [Philip. iii. 8.]

Is thy love to him a *rational* love, the effect of ferious thought, and deep conviction of his tranfcendent excellency? has the fpirit of God opened thy eyes, to fee that he is the *chief of ten thoufands, and altogether lovely?* and canft thou tell, *what* the church's *beloved is more than another's beloved?*

Is it a *conftant* and *fixed* love? not a fudden flafh, or tranfient paffion, but a rooted, fettled thing, a vigorous flame, which many *waters can't quench, nor the floods drown it?* and though thy love to fome dear creatures may unhappily be more paffionate; yet art thou come to a point, that thou wilt facrifice the deareft object, rather than part with *him whom thy foul loves?*—But to bring the matter to a more certain iffue; is thy love *practical?* this is an infallible teft; for my Lord

has

has faid, *ye are my friends, if ye do whatfoever I command you:* [Johh xv. 14.] doft thou count his *yoke eafy, and his burden light?* are none of his *commandments grievous?* doft thou delight to do his will, and haft thou chofe his *teftimonies as a heritage for ever?* doft thou find his love fweetly *conftraining* thee to the fevereft inftances of felf-denial? and art thou fully purpofed in a better ftrength than thy own, that thou wilt *follow the lamb whither-foever he goes,* whatever it cofts thee? If it be thus with thee, thou mayeft chearfully fay, *Lord, thou* that *knoweft all things, knoweft that I love thee* ·

And as a yet farther evidence, doft thou *love thy neighbour as thyfelf?* haft thou a *real* love for *all* men, and a *fpecial, peculiar* one for thy *fellow-chriftians?* is there no man, to whom thou doft not moft heartily wifh well, whatever provocations he has given thee, or injuries he has done thee? tho' thou haft many enemies, has no man an enemy of thee? if there are thofe that *hate* thee *with a cruel hatred,* canft thou appeal to GOD, that the hatred is not mutual and reciprocal? canft thou fincerely pray, *forgive our trefpaffes, as we forgive them that trefpafs againft us?*

And as to the *people of God,* doft thou *honour* and *delight* in them? hereby *we know that we have paffed from death to life, becaufe we love the brethren* · [1 John iii. 14.] doft thou love every foul, where thou feeft the image·

of

of Chriſt? is not thy love *confined* to thoſe of thy own party, or perſuaſion? but is it *unreſtrained* and large, as that *catholick church* of which thou art a member? does this love engage thee to all proper *acts of kindneſs* and expreſſions of brotherly love? doſt thou pity and help, to the utmoſt of thy power, all thoſe whom Chriſt calls brethren, with this view, that what thou doſt for them, terminates ultimately upon him, according to *Mat.* xxv? canſt thou read the *firſt epiſtle* of *John*, and thy heart not condemn thee?

I hope my love is *ſincere*——

‘ But, O my GOD, how *weak* and how
‘ *imperfect* is it! I even hate myſelf, that I
‘ can love thee no more. I abhor myſelf,
‘ that I love thy Chriſt no better; and bluſh
‘ to think that I am no more kindly affec-
‘ tioned to thoſe whom thou haſt loved
‘ with an everlaſting love; and with whom I
‘ hope to live and converſe for ever.

‘ My only comfort is, that I *would* love
‘ thee; I *deſire* to love thee; I *long* to love
‘ thee, even as thou wouldeſt be loved.
‘ Lord, kindle my ſpark into a flame, and
‘ let that flame be ſtrong and ſteady, and eſ-
‘ pecially grant that my *obedience* may prove
‘ my love to be of the right kind; *how can
‘ I ſay I love thee, if my heart be not right
‘ with thee?*——And for thy ſake, may I love
‘ my neighbour; eſpecially the happy mem-
‘ bers of that glorious family, to which it is
‘ my

' my higheſt honour to belong: O may I
' love them as myſelf, and in honour prefer
' them before myſelf, and think no office of
' love too mean for me to ſtoop to, in imi-
' tation of him, *who came not to be miniſtered*
' *unto, but to miniſter*; [Mat. xx. 28.] *this*
' *I pray, that my love may abound more and*
' *more*: [Philip. i. 9.] and being hearty and
' fervent in this requeſt, is, I hope, an evi-
' dence that I do truly love thee. Oh ! let
' me not be miſtaken, for Jeſus Chriſt his
' ſake. *Amen.*'

SECT. VII.

I Muſt alſo examine myſelf concerning my
new obedience. This I know is the *ultimate*
teſt of all my pretences : without it faith, repentance, love, &c. are empty names, and
inſignificant ſhadows. Is the will of GOD
my *law* ? his word my *rule* ? and his glory
the *end* of all my actions ? do I allow myſelf
in the commiſſion of no known ſin, or omiſ-
ſion of no known duty ? is it my conſtant care
to *keep a conſcience void of offence, both towards*
God and man ? can my *cloſet*, my *family*, my
ſhop, my *companions*, as well as the *public aſ-*
ſemblies of GOD's people, bear me witneſs,
that notwithſtanding my unallowed failings,
I do endeavour to walk in all the *ordinances*
and commandments of God blameleſs ? am I
willing to *know* my duty, and careful to *do*

it ? am I thankful for inſtruction, and reproof too; and do I count them my friends that tell me the truth ? are my remaining corruptions, and my many failings, matter of humiliation to me ? do I pray for daily *grace*, as *heartily* as for my daily *bread* ? and can I appeal to the ſearcher of hearts, that I am never more in earneſt, than when I pray that I may be *perfect in every good work, to do his will*; [Heb. xiii. 21.] that I may be cleanſed from all *filthineſs both of fleſh and ſpirit, and perfect holineſs, in the fear of the Lord*; [2 Cor. vii. 1.] that *I may be ſanctified wholly, and my whole ſpirit, ſoul and body, be preſerved blameleſs, to the coming of our Lord?* [1 Theſſ. v. 23.]

I hope it is *thus* with me *in ſome meaſure*——

‘ But, O my God, let me not be deceiv‘ ed ! If my obedience be feigned, or partial, ‘ or legal, if it do not exceed *that of the* ‘ *ſcribes and phariſees*, if I have a *form of god-* ‘ *lineſs without the power*, or *a name to live* ‘ *while I am dead*, diſcover to me the worſt ‘ of myſelf, that I may be upon a right ‘ bottom, and may get that *goſpel holineſs,* ‘ *without which I cannot ſee the Lord.* If ‘ there be a good work begun, O carry it ‘ on to the *day of Jeſus !* and let the ſolemn ‘ ordinance I am preparing for, be a means ‘ of my ſpiritual nouriſhment, and growth in grace. *Amen.*’

SECT. VIII.

I Hope I have *been impartial* in my felf-examinations.—And though upon review I find abundant matter for humiliation ; yet I cannot conclude myfelf a hypocrite, but muft entertain fome *good hope through grace,* that I am a *fincere,* though very *imperfect* Chriftian, and fhall be a *welcome* gueft at my Lord's table.

That which now remains, is, that I put myfelf in as *good* a *pofture* as may be, to meet my Lord at that folemnity, that I may not provoke his difpleafure, nor balk my own expectations. To this end I muft fee that every grace be in lively and vigorous *exercife,* left, having *in my flock a male, I fhould vow and facrifice to the Lord a corrupt thing.* [Mal. i. 14.]

I am fenfible, *faith* is a principal and leading grace : it is the *fubftance* (or confident expectation) *of things hoped for, and the evidence of things not feen ; without faith it is impoffible to pleafe God.* [Heb. xi. 1, 6.] I cannot queftion the *being* of a GOD, and the *certainty* of a *future* ftate, which are the great principles of *natural* religion, and prefuppofed to all *revealed.* I believe that *God is; and that he is the rewarder of all them that diligently feek him.* [Ibid.] But this is not enough ; my Lord has faid, *ye believe in God, believe alfo in me :* [John xiv. 1.] no knowledge of the

the *only true God* is fufficient to *eternal life*, while men are ignorant of *that Jefus Chrift whom he hath fent.* [John xvii. 3.] — Come then, O my foul, let thy faith in him be ftrong and lively! have I not abundant evidence, that Jefus is the *Meffiah*, the Chrift of G o d, that *him hath God the father fealed?* The *fcriptures* of the old teftament, *teftify* of him. [John vi. 27. and ver. 39.] To him *Mofes and all the Prophets bear witnefs.* [Acts x. 43] In him there was a full, and exact accomplifhment of every *promife*, and *prediction:* in him are the fubftance of all the *legal fhadows,* and to him referred all the *types, &c.* he was evidently the *promifed feed, the Shiloh,* the *branch, &c.* of the ancient fathers, who *waited for the confolation* of Ifrael. [Luke ii. 25.]

Confider, O my foul, what a glorious teftimony G o d bore to him by *a voice from heaven;* by vaft numbers of great publick and uncontefted *miracles;* and finally, by raifing him from the dead: of which he appointed competent *witneffes,* men of *ability* and *integrity:* who could not be impofed upon in fo plain a matter, and who could never be fuppofed to practife upon the world, becaufe there was no intereft in view that fhould engage them in fo bafe a defign; and it is utterly impoffible, that men in their wits fhould be guilty of the blackeft villany, in profpect of nothing but mifery and ruin——

Befides,

Besides, did not *God also bear them witness, both with signs and wonders, and divers miracles and gifts of the Holy Ghost?* [Heb. ii. 4.] To which may be added *this other* consideration, that *that doctrine* must needs be *from* God, which has so visible and peculiar a *tendency to make men* God-*like*, in the temper of their minds, and course of their actions: that gospel must needs be the *grace of God*, which *teaches* us so effectually, *that denying ungodliness and all worldly lusts, we should live soberly, righteously and godly in this present evil world.* [Tit. ii. 11, 12.] I find, by the records of past ages, and the observations I have made in the compass of my own acquaintance, that the *best christians* have been the *best men.* And, O my soul, canst thou not bear thine own testimony, that *the interest of* GOD *in thee* bears a constant proportion to the measure of *thy faith in Christ Jesus?* dost thou not always find, that, when thy *faith* is ready to *fail*, the good *things that remain are ready to die?* [Rev. iii. 2.] And on the contrary, is thy *heart* ever so *pure*, and thy *life* so clean, as when thy *faith* is *vigorous* and *lively?* Now, can any thing be more incredible, than that the great God should make use of an *imposture* to renew his own image upon the souls of men? I will as soon believe any absurdity, as that the most holy God should erect and support his kingdom in the world by a lye; and destroy the

interest

intereſt of the devil, by arts and methods perfectly helliſh and diabolical.

Come then, O my ſoul, be *ſtrong in faith, giving glory to God.* [Rom. iv. 20.] 'Tis true, believing is hard work; but conſider whence the *difficulties* ariſe; from a *corrupt heart,* and a *malicious enemy:* and let this thought be a farther evidence to the credibility of the doctrine of the croſs. Why ſhould a baſe heart and a buſy devil, make ſuch mighty oppoſition to the work of faith? If it were not the *work* of God, the *enemies* of God would never make ſuch efforts to hinder it. the devil would cheriſh his own creature; the world would love its own; and the fleſh would never expreſs ſuch a reluctancy againſt the goſpel, if it were not *ſpiritual* in its *tendency,* and *divine* in its *original.* Therefore, O my ſoul, let me form arguments out of difficulties, and pave my way with the very ſtumbling blocks that are thrown in it.

It is indeed an aſtoniſhing thought, that God ſhould become man, and *that* man ſhould die: *without controverſy, great is the myſtery of godlineſs,* &c. [1 Tim. iii. 16.] but let this not ſtagger thee. Conſider ſeriouſly that the more *awful* and *ſurprizing* the myſteries of the goſpel are, the more likely they are to be *from* God; who can ſcarce be ſuppoſed to declare any thing but what was extraordinary, and out of the reach of unaſſiſted

ed reason, with such a solemn pomp, and
train of mighty works, as were wrought to
confirm the mission of our Lord.   It would
have been matter of suspicion, if Christ and
his disciples had preached nothing but what
the *Pagan* philosophers taught, and the *Jew-
ish* doctors owned.   And it should recommend
the doctrine of Christ to a considering un-
prejudiced mind, that it was to the *Jews a
stumbling block, and to the Greeks foolishness.*
[1 Cor. 1. 23.]

Are not these things so ? Come then, O
my soul, *believe* and be *established.*

But, O wretched man that I am, *who shall
deliver me from this evil heart of unbelief ?* It is
not bare *external evidence* that will produce a
divine faith.   Faith I know is the work, the
mighty work of God, and produced in the
heart by no less power than that, which *raised
up Jesus from the dead ·* it is *not of ourselves :
it is the gift of God* [Eph. 1. 20. and 11. 8.]

' And therefore, O my God, I turn me
' unto thee, in whose hand my heart is, and
' who canst prevail against the united force·
' of my confederate enemies ; and not only
' begin, but carry on the *work of faith with·
' power.   I believe, Lord help my unbelief,*
' and *perfect that which is lacking in my faith.*
' Not only propose the object, but open my
' eyes that I may no more question what
' the gospel reveals, than what my eyes see ;
' that, *believing* in him whom *I do not see,*
' I may

' I may rejoice with joy unfpeakable and full of
' glory.'

SECT. IX.

I Muft alfo remember my Lord, in the exercife of *holy love*. And, O my foul, if
thou doft believe, thou can'ft not chufe
but love. View thy Lord in his glory and
beauty : confider him as the *brightnefs of his
father's glory, and the exprefs image of his perfon*; [Heb. i. 3.] think of him as the *chief
of ten thoufands, and altogether lovely*; as *one*,
whom all created brightnefs, fweetnefs, purity, and perfection, does but faintly reprefent; as *one*, in whom all that's lovely meets,
and triumphs; as *one*, whom the higheft *angels* worfhip, and by whom the moft fhining
feraphs are eclipfed; who yet adore, proftrate,
and veil before him with more exultation,
and rapture, than they would govern a thoufand worlds. Think of him as *one*, whofe
glories no thought can reach, nor words
exprefs; and whom the multitude of the
heavenly hoft will view with everlafting fur-
prize and admiration, as an object ever new,
and infinitely entertaining; and as defiring
no farther happinefs, than to *be with him
where he is, and behold his glory*. [John
xviii. 24.]

And, O my foul, confider that this glorious perfon, who is in himfelf fo infinitely
lovely,

lovely, has been infinitely *kind to thee !* need this be *proved*, or can the inftances of it be *forgotten ?* did not his love to thee appear beyond all contradiction, in his *incarnation, birth, fufferings,* and *death,* with all the circumftances of humility that attended his paffage thro' this *vale of tears, this wafte and howling wildernefs,* to that *better country,* where he is ftill mindful of his people, as *ever living to make interceffion for them ?* he loved thee before thou or time were : he loved thee, when he was *on earth,* with a love *ftronger than death, which many waters could not quench, nor floods drown ;* he loves thee now he is *in heaven ;* and tho' he be exalted to the higheft dignity, far above all principalities and powers, and *fits at the right hand of God* as *Lord of all,* yet haft thou the fame place in his heart, and the fame fhare in his affectionate remembrances. Long abfence, great diftance, high preferment, multiplicity of affairs, which impair common friendfhip, have no influence there : *having loved his own which were in the world,* he does and will love them *to the end ;* [John xiii. 1.] and that with a love more conftant, fteady and regular, than the revolutions of the heavenly bodies, and the fettled *courfe of nature.* Nor is this love of his an *empty* name. Confider, O my foul, the glorious effects of it. 'Tis a love big with bleffings ; bleffings which no tongue can reprefent, and nothing here below refemble,

ble, but with a great deal of faintnefs and imperfection: he has *loved me and wafhed me from my fins in his blood*: [Rev. i. 5.] he was *made fin for me, that I might be made the righteoufnefs of God, in him*: [2 Cor. v. 21.] *he was wounded for my tranfgreffions, and bruifed for mine iniquities; the chaftifement of my peace was upon him, and with his ftripes I am healed*: [Ifa. liii. 5] *being juftified by faith, I have peace with God through him*: [Rom. v. 1.] and by him accefs with boldnefs to the *throne of grace*. [Heb. iv. 16.] To his expenfive love, as the meritorious caufe, I owe my *regeneration*, that I am *begotten again to a lively hope*: my *adoption*, that I am called a *child of God*: my *fanctification*, my *peace, comfort* and *joy*; and finally, my *hopes of eternal life*; which is all that heart can wifh, and ten thoufand thoufand times more; for *the things which God hath prepared for them that love him, have not entered into the heart of man*. [1 Cor ii. 9.]

Nor let me, O my foul, forget who is the unworthy object of all this glorious love; *what am I, and what is my father's houfe*, that I fhould be thus *highly favoured?* that the prince of life, the living God, fhould fet his heart upon fuch a *dead dog*; that a vile *worm*, finful *duft* and *afhes*, fhould be fo regarded by him, whom *all the angels worfhip*, whom the whole creation obeys; and in comparifon of whom all created beings are

are *as a drop of a bucket, and the small dust of a balance ' nothing, yea less than nothing, and vanity !* behold *what manner of love* is this' *expression* is at a loss, and *silent admiration* must supply its place.

Now, does not this love deserve love? whence is it, O my soul, that thou art no more affected? that in these *musings the fire burns* no more? one would think, that, upon such a subject, serious thoughts should exalt even a spark of love into a flame of transport and ecstasy ' and whence is all this' coldness?

Oh it is from my *evil heart of unbelief !* the things are so great that they even exceed belief ' but let me consider that *God's ways are not as ours, nor his thoughts as ours, but more above them than the heavens are above the earth !* [Isa. lv. 8, 9.] and that his benefits are in suitable proportion to his own greatness. Royal favours use to be vast and magnificent: they give *like kings*; and what less can be expected from the *King of kings*, the infinite majesty of heaven and earth, than what he has pleased to appoint for his favourites ' and the more *mean* the *objects* of his love are, the more *glorious* his *bounty !* the lower his goodness stoops, the higher it rises ' but that it should stoop so low as me, the least, and *less than the least of all saints*, nay the very *chief of sinners*; this, this staggers my faith, and makes me ready to cry out; " 'Tis impos-
" sible,

" fible, it can never be, that God fhould
" love fuch a worm, fuch a devil as I am!
" a vile traitor that have broken his laws,
" defpifed his grace, *quenched* his *fpirit*,
" *trampled under foot his fon!* an ungracious,
" *dog*, that has turned his *grace into wanton-*
" *nefs*, and continued in fin in fpite of all re-
" claiming methods! a backfliding, treach-
" erous, perjured beaft! and under the con-
" victions of all this, no more moved than
" a clod, or a rock! a ftupid hard-hearted
" finner!"——this I muft confefs I find difficult to believe; and when I can hope, I
wonder at myfelf that I can venture to do it;
and adore the grace and mercy of God,
that I have not long ago been a *Cain*, or
a *Judas*, or at leaft a *Spira*, a *magor miffa-*
bib, a terror to myfelf and all about me, by
reafon of the blacknefs and horror of my
defpair!

And yet here infinite *mercy*, and infinite
merit, are a relief! I will believe that there
is mercy for the *worft*, becaufe God has faid
it; and I won't venture to except myfelf, becaufe God has not done it: *all things are pof-*
fible with God; he can *forgive frankly* ten
thoufand talents, as well as a few pence: and
he will forgive *manifold iniquities*, and *mighty*
fins, to every penitent, humble, willing foul.
[*Vid.* Luke vii. 42, *&c.*] I muft not deny the
grace of God; and therefore, if I do avouch
this character, confequently I muft believe.

And

And then how can I chuse but love? Oh my soul, fall with the lowest prostrations at the feet of thy dearest *Jesus*; and if thou canst do no better, express thy love by *sighs* and *blushes*, that thou canst love him no more.

' But, Lord, I may expostulate with my-
' self till I am weary, if thy *grace* be with-
' held, and thy *spirit* denied! *O shed abroad*
' *thy love in my heart, by the Holy Ghost given*
' *unto me* strike this rock and it shall melt;
' breathe upon this clod, and it will warm;
' *draw* me, and I shall *run after thee.* I can-
' not say that I *do* love thee; but I am sure
' I can say, that I *would* love thee: this
' *thou knowest*, that *knowest all things.* I can
' appeal to thee, that, if I might have my
' wish, I would love thee better than any
' *saint* on earth, yea, than any *angel* in hea-
' ven does. I had rather love thee as I
' ought to love thee, than be master of all
' the treasures on earth; rather than have all
' the monarchs of it at my feet; rather
' than have all that the world admires at my
' disposal. I had rather (Lord *thou knowest!*)
' die in an ecstasy of holy love, and breathe
' out my soul into the arms of the holy Je-
' sus, than live ten millions of years; yea
' to all eternity, in the fulness of all created
' enjoyments. O my God, is not this a re-
' quest after thine own heart, when I pray
' that I may love thee with all my soul; and

2   ' that

' that I may not be moft flat and heavy, cold
' and lifeleſs, at that *ſolemnity*, where are the
' memorials of the choiceſt and moſt glori-
' ous love, that was ever known or heard
' of ?'

SECT. X.

I Muſt alſo, at the Lord's table, be in a
penitent frame.　The remembrance of
my Lord's dying love muſt melt my
heart into a kindly *ſorrow* for thoſe *ſins* which
wounded and ſlew him　*His ſoul* was *made an
offering for* my *ſin*; [Iſa. liii. 10.] and ſhall
not *my heart* bleed at the thought of that *bitter cup*, in which my ſins were deadly ingre-
dients, and which for my ſake he drank off
even to the very diegs ?　O my ſoul, when I
remember my Saviour, I muſt penitently remember my ſins, from which he died to ſave
me.　My ſins ! how wide a field ! how vaſt
a ſubject ! I am amazed, and ſtagger at the
general proſpect, and muſt be ſwallowed up
and loſt in *particulars* ! where ſhall I begin,
and where ſhall I end ?　Indeed I may begin
at the root.　*Behold ! I was ſhapen in iniquity,
and in ſin did my mother conceive me* ! [Pſal.
li. 5.] but the numerous branches exceed cal-
culation ! *I know not the numbers thereof ! the
commandment of God is exceeding broad*; and
in proportion to it I muſt eſtimate my guilt !
what commandment have I not broken ?　in
what

what inftance have I not offended? as to my
fins of *ignorance* and *common frailties*, I muft
only figh and fay, *who can underftand his errors?* [Pfal. xix. 12.] for to remember and
lament my *groffer* follies, will be a *long* as
well as *forrowful* employment, and take up
more time than my circumftances can allow.
But, O my foul, I charge thee mourn over
the more heinous offences of thy life: read
over thy *calendar*, and drop a tear upon the
black days there *.

> N. *Here call forrowfully to mind fuch par-
> ticular fins, as have been more efpecially
> heinous.*

And tho' I. hope God has forgiven thee,
yet, O my foul, never forgive thyfelf. O
what fhall I fay? *I blufh and am afhamed to
lift up my face to thee, my God!* [Ezr. ix. 6]
I could have no peace, no patience, no hope,
were it not for fuch a word as that · *the blood
of Jefus Chrift, his fon, cleanfes from all fin.*
[John i. 7.]
I would alfo particularly review my converfation, fince the *laft facrament.* And here
I can find matter enough for fhame and grief.
Oh! wretch that I am, how unfuitable has
my converfation been to the profeffion and
engagements I fo lately made, and the fweet
experiences I fo much rejoiced in, and feemed
fo thankful for?

* *Bp.* Wilkins.

C   N. *Here*

N. Here fix your thoughts upon the groffer follies of the preceding month.

Was *fuch* an *action* becoming what thou didft fo lately, at the Lord's table, pretend and promife? was fuch a management worthy of a *chriftian*, and becoming a *communicant?* did the indulgence of fuch a flefhly luft become a *difciple* of the holy *Jefus*, the immaculate *lamb of God?* did it become a fheep of *Chrift*'s flock, to wallow like a fwine in that mire? was that *pride*, that *paffion*, that *malice*, *envy*, and *uncharitablenefs*, fuitable to thy folemn profeffion of retaining to him, who came to *deftroy the works of the devil?* [1 John iii. 8.] *Remember and be confounded, and never open thy mouth any more becaufe of thy fhame!* [Ezek xvi. 63.] *Surely I am more brutifh than any man, and have not the underftanding of a man!* [Prov. xxx. 2.]

And, O my foul, fhall not the *time paft fuffice* thee, [1 Pet. iv. 3.] to have acted fo inconfiftently and unaccountably? furely it becomes me to fay, *If I have done iniquity, I will do fo no more.* Let thefe be my fincere *refolutions*; and let me, at the *Lord's table*, bind myfelf in frefh bonds, that my future *walk* fhall be more circumfpect; that my *devotions* fhall be more regular; my *dealings* more juft; my *charity* more extenfive; and my *whole converfation* more fpiritual.

‘ O my God, this is my full purpofe; but
‘ let me not want that *grace*, which alone

' *is sufficient for me :* give me true repentance ;
' let me take up sincere resolutions ; and let
' the uprightness of my heart in both appear
' in a suitable behaviour for time to come.
' *So be it,* for *Jesus* sake.

CHAP. V.

The Christian *at the* Lord's Table.

SECT. I.

NOW, O my soul, the good hand of
God upon thee has brought thee into
his house, and set thee at his table ! behold
all things are ready ! see to it that thou be
ready to meet and entertain thy Lord.

' *Awake, O North wind, and come thou*
' *South, blow upon my garden, that the spices*
' *thereof may flow out. let my beloved come*
' *into his garden, and eat his pleasant fruits.*'
[Sol. Song iv. 16.]

When *the king comes in to see his guests,*
' may I not be *the man* that wants a *wedding*
' *garment ?*' [Mat. xxii. 11.]

'Tis an awful solemnity ! O my soul, approach with *reverence and godly fear.*

This is none other but the house of God, and
this is the gate of heaven : [Gen. xxviii. 17.]
let my frame be suitable, *spiritual and hea-*
venly.

' O my God, keep off the tempter, keep

' out

' out the world, keep down my corruption.'

‘ Let no luft defile : let no bufinefs engage : let no impertinent thought divert
‘ my mind. *Unite my heart*; and let it be
‘ intent and fixed in thee.

‘ Thy *grace*, O Lord, *is fufficient* for me :
let thy *ftrength* be *made perfect* in my *weaknefs.*

‘ *Work in me both to will and do : ftrengthen*
‘ *me with all might, by thy fpirit, in the inward*
‘ *man.*

‘ Call up my faith and love, and every
‘ proper grace, into lively and vigorous ex-
‘ ercife.

‘ *Bleffed Jefus, without thee I can do nothing.*
‘ *I can do all things through Chrift ftrengthening*
‘ *me. Draw me, I will run after thee.*

SECT. II.

While the Minifter *is* breaking *the* Bread.

THUS was the *body* of my *Lord* broken ! *It pleafed the Lord to bruife him,
and put him to grief !*

He was bruifed for our iniquities ! [Ifai. iii.
5, 10]

O let me view the reprefentation of his
broken body, with a *broken* heart, *and a contrite
fpirit !*

Hard indeed muft that heart be, which
fuch a fight will not affect !

Methinks I fee his precious body fcourged
and pierced ! it is an affecting thought, that
perfect

perfect innocence should be thus treated ! but when I consider, that this innocent lamb was at the same time *God over all blessed for ever*, and that he underwent all this *for me*, what must my heart be, if it be not affected !

And while his *body* was thus bruised, the *iron* enter'd into his *soul*. Who can imagine what our *Lord* felt, when he cried out, *My God, my God, why hast thou forsaken me ?*

See here what an *evil and bitter thing sin* is ; and how abominable in the sight of *God*; when no *less* a sacrifice could appease incensed Justice !

Here is grace ! here is love ! that God should *prepare* his own son a *body* ; and that in that *body*, he *should bear our sins on the tree* [1 Pet. ii. 24.]

SECT. III.

While the Minister *is* pouring out *of the* Wine.

THUS was my *Lord's blood shed for me. We are redeemed not with corruptible things, as silver or gold; but with the precious blood of Christ, as of a lamb without blemish and without spot* [1 Pet. i. 18, 19.]

If the blood of bulls and goats sanctifieth to the purifying of the flesh; how much more shall the blood of him, who thro' the eternal spirit offered himself without spot to God, purge your consciences from dead works, to serve the living God? [Heb. ix. 13, 14.]

C 3

Oh

Oh let me view a bleeding *Jesus* with a *bleeding heart*.

Behold the *fountain set open for sin and for uncleanness! The blood of Jesus Christ cleanses from all sin.* [1 John 1. 7.]

Approach, apply, O my soul, wash and be clean. *purge with* this *hyssop, and* thou *shalt be clean*, *wash* in this laver, *and* thou *shalt be whiter than the snow.* [Psal. li 7]

What may not be expected from the *blood of God?* the *blood* of him, that was GOD? [*Vide* Acts xx. 28]

Oh how freely did he let out his blood! view with transport those streams of love; and think how much thou owest to him, who so freely laid down his life for thee!

‘ Oh my GOD, enlarge my heart in love to
‘ such a friend, and never let my heart be
‘ *straitned* towards him, who opened his veins
‘ and so *freely* bled and died for me.

‘ May my eye affect my heart; and may
‘ I with the utmost tenderness remember what
‘ evidences he has given of his love to me.——
‘ *Was ever love like this!*

SECT. IV.
Taking *the* Bread, *&c.*

BLeſſed *Jeſus,* thou art *that bread of life:* thy broken body is food for ſouls. Oh! let me by faith *eat* and *live, eat and never die!* [John vi. 48, 49, 50.]

' When *Judas took the ſop, Satan entered into him:* Lord grant, that, as I receive this bread, Chriſt may enter, and take an eter- nal poſſeſſion of my ſoul!'

Now, O my ſoul, take a whole *Jeſus,* with a whole *heart,* for a whole *ſalvation.*

Lord, I am not worthy thou ſhouldeſt come un- der my roof.

I am indeed infinitely *unworthy,* but I hope, through grace, not utterly *unwilling.*

O were but my appetite to this ſpiritual food equal to my need of it; how *wide* would my ſoul *open her mouth,* and how full would ſhe be *filled!* [Pſal. lxxxi. 10.]

' Oh thou, who haſt provided bread, give me an appetite, and *abundantly bleſs my proviſion!*

' *Lord, increaſe my faith!*

' O let this bread be bleſt to my ſpiritual nouriſhment, and growth in grace!

' O that I may *receive* out of Chriſt's *ful- neſs, even grace for grace!'* [John i. 16.]

By theſe royal dainties, may my lean and withering ſoul become *fat and flouriſhing!* [Pſal. xcii. 14.]

His

His flesh is meat indeed. [John vi. 55.]

O my soul, accept and resign ; take a *Jesus,* and surrender thyself. *My Lord and my God, I am thine, save me*

I avouch the Lord this day to be my God: [Deut. xxvi. 17.] *his I am, and him I'll serve.* [Acts xxvii 23.]

Blessed be the God and Father of our Lord Jesus Christ, who hath blessed us with all spiritual blessings, in heavenly places *in Christ.* [Eph. i. 3]

Blessed be God for *Jesus Christ*

Thanks be to God for his unspeakable gift.

SECT. V.

Taking *the* Cup, *&c.*

THIS *Cup is the New Testament in my* Lord's *blood.* [1 Cor xi. 25]

I will take the cup of salvation, and pay my vows.

Christ's blood is drink indeed ! [John vi. 55]

I take this *cup of blessing,* and O adored be his love that was *made a curse* for me, [Gal. iii. 13] that he might fill this cup with blessing.

O how freely did my Lord *drink of the brook in the way !* [Psal. cx. 7.] Remember, O my soul, *that* love, which made him say, *The cup which my Father hath given me, shall I not drink it ?* [John xviii. 11.] It was a *bitter* cup to *him,* and yet he drank the very

dregs

dregs of it.—It is a cup of *blessing* to *me*, and shall I not *chearfully* drink of *it in remembrance of him?*

Blessed Jesus, *thou hast drank at the hand of the Lord the cup of his fury. Thou hast drunken the dregs of the cup of trembling, and wrung them out ;* [Isai. li. 17] and hast put into my hand this *cup of consolation. Behold what manner of love!*

O precious *blood, that cleanses from all sin!*

Drink, O my soul, and remember *Jesus.*

Drink, and mourn over thy sins and follies.

Drink, and receive thy pardon.

Drink, and renew thy covenant.

Drink, and *forget thy sorrows.*

Drink, and forgive thy enemies.

Drink, and triumph over the adversaries of thy soul.

Drink, and *rejoice in hope of the glory of God.*

Blessed *Jesus,* I will *remember thy love more than wine.* [Sol. Song i. 4.]

Unto him that hath loved us, and washed us from our sins in his blood, and hath made us kings and priests unto God, and his Father ; to him be glory and dominion, for ever and ever. Amen. [Rev. 1. 5, 6.]

Blessed be God for *Jesus Christ.*

Thanks be unto God for his unspeakable gift.

SECT. VI.

At the Conclusion *of the Ordinance.*

*W*Orthy *is the lamb that was slain to receive power, and riches, and wisdom, and strength, and honour, and glory, and blessing.*

Blessing, honour, glory, and power, be unto him that sitteth upon the throne, and unto the lamb, for ever and ever. [Rev. v. 12, 13.]

How amiable are thy tabernacles, O Lord of hosts ! blessed are they that dwell in thy house ; *a day in thy courts is better than a thousand ; I had rather be a door-keeper in the house of my God, than to dwell in the tents of wickedness.* [Psal. lxxxiv. 1, 4, 10.]

And, O my soul, if this hour has been so sweet, while *I beheld the king in his glory, and the land which is afar off,* tho' it were *as in a glass darkly,* what will an eternity in heaven be ! when *I shall see him as he is, and know as I am also known !* when I shall *be with him where he is, and behold his glory !* make haste, O my beloved.

Thus I must remember my Lord *till he comes :* blessed be God for such an ordinance ! But O that *my soul* could *even break for the longing I have* for that second coming ; when *he shall appear to them that look for him, without sin, unto salvation.* [Heb. ix. 28]

He has said, *Behold I come quickly ,* even so, Lord Jesus, come quickly ; [Rev. xxii. 20.] in

the

the mean time, O my ſoul, remember *where*
thou haſt been, and *what* thou haſt been doing' *Thou haſt opened thy mouth to the Lord,
and muſt not go back :* thou haſt bound thy ſoul
with an oath : *thou haſt ſworn, and muſt perform it, to keep his righteous judgments.*

Thou haſt *avouched, this day, the Lord to
be thy God :* be *true* to him : let him *alone* be
exalted in thy ſoul. be *for* him, and not for
another.

' Now, O my God, I bleſs thee for the
' liberty of thy houſe : I bleſs thee for the
' aids of thy ſpirit : the ſhame of my miſ-
' behaviour I take to myſelf; but all the
' praiſe I give to thee. Oh by thy grace
' help me, as *I have received Chriſt Jeſus the
' Lord, ſo to walk in him,* [Col. ii. 6.] *that
' where he is, I,* his unworthy ſervant, *may
' alſo be. Amen* and *Amen.*

CHAP. VI.

The Chriſtian *in his* Retirements, *after
the Lord's Supper.*

SECT. I.

When the Ordinance *has been* comfortable.

Bleſs the Lord, O my Soul, and all that is
within me bleſs his holy name · bleſs the
Lord, O my Soul, and forget not all his benefits;

who

who crowneth thee with loving-kindnefs, and tender mercies · who fatisfieth thy mouth with good things. [Pfal. ciii 1, &c.] How thankful ought I to be, that the doors of God's *houfe* have been open to me, and that I have had the freedom of his *table ! whence is this to me*, that I, who have long ago deferved to be fhut up among the *fpirits in prifon*, and fed with the *bread* of *affliction*, and *water* of *affliction*, fhould be admitted a gueft at *fuch* a feaft ! A *feaft of fat things, and of wine upon the lees, well refined !* that I fhould *fee the king in his glory*, and *fit with him at his table* ; who might have expected ere now to have been banifhed for ever from his prefence, and have heard that killing word, *See my face no more !*

Bleffed be God, that he let me live to fee this *day*, this *joyful day !* that I was not prevented by a furprifing ftroke, and led captive by death into the chambers of that *houfe appointed for all living*, long before this !

Bleffed be his name, that I have been fuffered to live no longer in the *neglect* of fuch a fweet and profitable *ordinance* ! that he convinced me of my *duty*, brought me to *refolve*, and confirmed my refolutions . fo that, in fpite of all the malice of Satan, I have *given* up *myfelf to the Lord*, and to his church, *by the will of God* [2 Cor. viii. 5] This is what I had defigned once and again, *but Satan hindred !* bleffed be the *captain of my falvation, on*, that he has hindered no longer! that all the mighty hofts of objections, he had muftered up, could not deter me from my duty; that I was *willing in the day of thy power!* [Pfal. cx. 3.]

Bleffed be God that my *natural floth*, and *love of eafe*, did not make me balk a duty, which requires induftry and laborious application, in preparing for it: that my *eagernefs after the world* did not make me grudge the time, which a worthy communicant muft redeem from his fecular affairs, for this folemn fervice: efpecially, that my unbelieving *doubts* and *fcruples*, *fears* and *jealoufies*, did not put me by my duty, under apprehenfions of unfitnefs and unworthinefs.

I am alfo bound to praife him, for the affiftance of his holy fpirit and grace; that my mind was in any meafure compofed; that the *defire of my foul was towards him, and the remembrance of his name;* that I have reafon to hope I was fincere, and acted in the integrity of my heart: tho' I muft blufh that I did no better; I muft blefs him I did fo well; *not I, but the grace of God with me! not unto us, Lord, not unto us!*

But, O my foul, don't let thy gratitude be only in *general* terms: review the whole affair, and be *particular* in the acknowledgments. There may be great love expreffed in circumftances feemingly minute; the

the recollection of which may afford great delight, and does demand a grateful refentment.

I am bound to blefs my GOD, that by his kind providence he *brought me* to that *banqueting-houfe, where his banner over me was love*, [Sol Song ii. 4] that the doors of *his fanctuary* were open ; that my lot is not caft in thofe places, where the *fynagogues of God* are deftroyed, his minifters *driven into corners*, and *devout* fouls forced to gather the *heavenly manna*, their fpiritual food, with the *peril of their lives*. Bleffed be GOD, that by the favour of our *governors* (whom the Lord blefs and preferve !) we may affemble together, *and none make us afraid :* that he *prepares a table for us in the prefence of our enemies :* [Pfal. xxiii. 5.] and if the fons of *Belial* malign and curfe us, they cannot deftroy us, nay dare not difturb us. Bleffed be GOD, they can't infult us, and fay, *where is now your God ?* we may now go *with the multitude, go to the houfe of God with the voice of joy and praife, with the multitude that keep holy-day.* [Pfal. xlii. 3, 4.] Bleffed be his name, that we, who can boldly avouch ourfelves to be of thofe that *are quiet in the land,* [Pfal xxxv. 20.] are allowed to enjoy our native rights, and are not by the rulers counted difturbers of the publick peace, or *hurtful to kings.* [Ezr. iv. 15.]

I muft

I muſt alſo praiſe him, that no *evil befel* me, nor *plague came nigh my dwelling*, which might have *ſhut me up*, tho' the doors of his houſe were open: that *my houſe* was not ſhut up, and a *Lord have mercy* writ over it: that no *evil diſeaſe cleaved to me*; [Pſal. xli. 8.] nor were my *loins filled with a loathſome diſeaſe*; [Pſal. xxxviii. 7.] which would have confined me to my bed, or chamber, and forbid my going up to the houſe of the Lord: that the *ſecret of God was upon my tabernacle*, and no ſore *calamity* befel me, that would have unhinged my mind, and made me uncapable of attending at the *ordinance*, with any compoſure and devotion. Bleſſed be God, that I had not occaſion for *Aaron*'s apology, when he had neglected to eat the ſin-offering in the holy place, *&c.* and *Moſes* expoſtulated with him upon it: *ſuch things have befallen me, and if I had eaten the ſin-offering to-day, ſhould it have been accepted in the ſight of the Lord?* [Levit. x. 19.] Eſpecially I would be thankful, that GOD did not withdraw his ſpirit, unchain the devil, and let looſe my corruption, ſo that being *overtaken with* ſome heinous *fault*, or *harraſſed with* ſome grievous *temptation*, I ſhould not have dared to approach to the *jealous* GOD in that *holy* ordinance; but my *place* muſt needs have been *empty*, becauſe an accuſing devil, and condemning conſcience, would clamour and ſay, *he is not clean, ſurely he is not clean!* [1 Sam xx. 26.]

I would

I would alſo praiſe my GOD, that I was not diſappointed by his hand upon the *mini-ſter*, the *ſteward* of theſe *myſteries:* that ſick-neſs or other calamities did not diſable him for his maſter's ſervice: that GOD was with him, according to his kind promiſe: that *Chriſt Jeſus was with his ſpirit*, and gave him the *tongue of the learned* to ſpeak a *word in ſeaſon.* How *awfully* did he *warn* us, that we ſhould not preſume to approach without the *wedding-garment !* how *ſweetly* did he *encourage* every devout and willing ſoul, to come with *boldneſs to the throne of grace*, and by faith to *draw water out of the wells of ſal-vation !* how *pathetically* did he *repreſent* the ſufferings of our Lord ! how *earneſtly* preſs *faith in his blood, and conformity to his death !* how *paſſionately did he recommend* his example, and *encourage* univerſal obedience, by diſ-playing the happineſs of thoſe that ſerve and follow him; who ſhall be *with him where he is, and behold his glory !* how fervently did he *pray* for the effuſion of the *Holy Spirit* upon every ſincere ſoul ! that GOD would *remem-ber us*, from the greateſt to the leaſt, *with the love which he bears to his own, and viſit us with his ſalvation*; that never a communi-cant at that table might be *myſſing* at the *right hand of Chriſt* another day ! that we might all *ſit down with* Abraham, Iſaac *and* Jacob, *in the kingdom of God*, and enter into *that reſt which remains for the people of God !*

Bleſſed

Bleſſed be God, that his mouth was not ſhut nor his ſpirit ſtraitned, as a juſt puniſhment of my ſins; whereby I have provoked him to abridge me of thoſe privileges I have ſo wretchedly miſimproved!

I muſt alſo bleſs his name, that he *did not deny his grace,* nor *withhold his ſpirit,* when I approached his table: altho' my preparations were ſo ſhort, ſo vaſtly below the ſtandard of the *ſanctuary,* and my whole management ſadly defective, nevertheleſs I hope I did meet with *him, whom my ſoul loves:* and the kindneſs of my Lord exceeded my expectations, as well as my deſerts. Bleſſed be GOD, it did not fare with me according to the preſages of my guilty miſgiving heart! I expected *killing frowns,* and to my great ſurpriſe was welcomed with *reviving ſmiles; he lifted up the light of his countenance upon me,* ſpoke good and comfortable words to me, and ſent me *away with mirth, and with ſongs, with tabret, and with harp.* [Gen. xxxi. 27.]

I will praiſe him, that he *helped my unbelief:* that, tho' I am *of little faith,* it was not to ſeek; when it ſhould be in exerciſe I would affectionately remember his kindneſs, in enabling me to *realize* inviſible things, that, when I ſaw the *elements,* I could look *thro'* them to the *bleſſed object* they were appointed to repreſent: tho' I am apt to be like unbelieving *Thomas,* yet *then* (through my Saviour's viour's adorable condefcenfion) I was *not faithlefs, but believing.* [John xx. 27.] He fo difcovered himfelf to my foul, that I could not forbear faying, *My Lord and my God!* I thought, I no more doubted, that *Jefus* was the *Meffiah,* him *whom God the Father fealed;* than if I had been by, *when there came fuch a voice to him from the excellent glory;* " *This* " *is my beloved Son, in whom I am well pleafed.*" I thought I as firmly believed his dying upon the crofs for *my* fins, as though I had been prefent at the awful fpectacle; as tho' I had flood by with the *blelfed virgin,* and the *beloved difciple.* [John xix. 25.] I faw by faith his body broken, and his blood flow; what inward agonies his countenance expref-fed, when he cried out, " *My God, my God,* " *why haft thou forfaken me?*" And with how glorious a mixture of majefty, love, and forrow he looked; when, having faid, *It is finifhed, he bowed his head, and gave up the ghoft.* [Ver. 30.]

I was enabled, without any hefitation, to believe, that as he died, fo he *rofe again, according to the fcriptures·* [1 Cor. xv. 4.] that, tho' he *was dead, he is alive, and lives for evermore.* [Rev. 1. 18.] I was almoft, in my own mind, a witnefs of his *afcenfion;* doubting no more of it, than if I had been among the *men of* Galilee, when *he was taken up, and a cloud received him out of their fight.*

fight. [Acts i. 9.] I was as firmly perſuaded of his *ſitting at the right hand of God*, there pleading the cauſe, and managing the affairs of his church; as if my *eyes had ſeen the king in his beauty, and the land which is far off*. [Iſa. xxxiii. 17.] Yea I could, I thought, look for his *ſecond appearance*, (which is to be *without ſin unto ſalvation*) with as much confidence, as if I had heard the two angels ſay, *Why ſtand ye here gazing up unto heaven? this ſame Jeſus which is taken up from you into heaven, ſhall come in like manner as ye have ſeen him go up into heaven*. [Acts i. 11.]

Yea, bleſſed be God, I was enabled to believe in this *Jeſus* as *my* Saviour. I was encouraged to ſay, this *body* was broken for *me*; this *blood* was ſhed for *me*: the *Son of God loved* me, *and gave himſelf for* me. [Gal. ii. 20.] And tho' I had a deep ſenſe of my own unworthineſs, and had manifold iniquities and mighty ſins to mourn over; yet (praiſed be his name) I was borne above my uſual fears and ſcruples, and by a holy violence, as it were, obliged to believe *in hope*, tho' *againſt hope*. [Rom. iv. 18.] I ſaw myſelf *vile* and *baſe* as hell, one of the worſt and chief of ſinners: and yet I durſt not *deſpair*, becauſe I had that word ſet home, *the blood of Chriſt cleanſes from all ſin*. [1 John i. 7] My dear Lord ſeemed to ſmile, and ſay, *Be of good cheer, be not afraid*,

it

it is I. [Mark vi. 50.] *Come unto me, ye that are weary, and heavy laden :* [Mat. xi. 28.] *and him that cometh unto me I will in nowise cast out.* [John vi. 37.] *Whosoever will, let him take the water of life freely.* [Rev. xxii. 17.]

Indeed my unbelieving heart was ready to say, *How can these things be?* can such a worm be the object of everlasting love? can such a vile polluted wretch pretend relation to, and interest in the holy *Jesus,* and expect admission into his holy hill? I was like *Jacob,* when he heard the news of *Joseph's* being alive, the Lord of *Egypt; his heart fainted, for he believed them not.* [Gen. xlv. 26.] But my spirit was revived, when my Lord shewed me the provisions which he had made for my going to possess the kingdom : And when I was helped to consider, that nothing is too great to be expected from infinite mercy, thro' infinite merits , blessed be God, I could cry out, *Lord, I believe, help thou mine unbelief.*

I must also adore and bless him, that *his love was shed abroad in my heart,* [Rom. v. 5.] in a degree beyond what I could have expected ; considering what a rock of ice, what a stupid, senseless thing this heart is. *I beheld* my Lord's *glory,* and could scarce forbear crying out aloud ; *This is my friend, this is my beloved, O ye daughters of Jerusalem.* [Sol. Song, v. 16.] I thought,
I saw

I saw him, as the *church* describes him; [Sol. Song, chap. v.] and could heartily join in that acclamation, *Yea, he is altogether lovely.* O how did I wish for nearer access to him, and clearer views of him! *My soul did thirst for God, for the living God: yea, as the hart panteth after the water-brooks, so did my soul pant after him.* [Psal. xlii. 1, 2.] I could have been even willing to have died in an ecstasy of love, that I might not have lost the sight of so glorious an object to all eternity.

O how did the tokens of his expensive love affect my soul, and fill me with gratitude! I thought, I could have died a thousand deaths for him, who *loved me and gave himself for me.* And Oh may I never forget, how ashamed and confounded I was then, to think of the sins and miscarriages of my past life; when I called to remembrance some of the many omissions and commissions, that are upon record in my conscience, how did my *heart smite* me? Oh, thought I, *is this thy kindness to thy friend! dost thou thus requite the Lord, O foolish creature, and unwise!* are these suitable returns to such amazing love? for which of his good works has he been thus treated, so neglected, so affronted by thee? is it not *high time* for me to *awake out of sleep,* to take up more firm and steady resolutions of better obedience? sure the *time past shal lsuffice* to have acted so unworthy

thy

thy of a *christian*, and of a *man*; yea to have debafed myfelf below the *beafts that perifh*: for *the ox knows his owner, and the afs his mafter's crib*. [Ifa. i. 3.]

Therefore I offer up my folemn thankf-giving to GOD, that he has by his fpirit and grace enabled me thus to *believe* and *love*; to *repent* and *refolve*. It is *he* has *worked in me both to will and to do*; and *his* fhall be the praife: elfe it had been with me as at other times, when to my fhame I muft own I went to the table *dull*, and returned *ftupid*, I went *dejected*, and returned *difconfolate*; when the whole of my performance was mere *bodily exercife*, which I found *profited nothing*. I muft afcribe it to his grace, that it was better with me than ufual; for, let others pretend what they will, for my part I find that I *am not fufficient of myfelf* to any thing fpiritually good: *in me, that is, in my flefh, dwells no good thing*.

'Now, O my GOD, accept my thankful
' acknowledgments: let me keep a fenfe of
' thy love ever frefh upon my foul: and ef-
' pecially help me to *walk worthy* of my pro-
' feffion and privileges; let me never *tread*
' *under foot the Son of God, nor count the blood*
' *of the covenant, wherewith I am fanctified, an*
' *unholy thing*. [Heb. x. 29.] *Amen*. For
' *Jefus fake*.'

SECT. II.

When the Ordinance *has* not anſwered
Expectation.

I Have been at the *table* of my Lord;
where he uſes to meet and bleſs his people. I went with raiſed hopes that (tho' infinitely unworthy) I ſhould have communion
with the Father and his Son Jeſus Chriſt;
[1 John i. 3] that I ſhould be richly entertained, and return rejoicing: but alas! how
ſadly am I diſappointed! *I came to the pits and
found no water!* I am *returned with my veſſels
empty!* I am *aſhamed and confounded!* [Jer. xiv.
3.] I had prepared a *ſong of praiſe*, and thought
to have cloſed the *feſtival* with *Hoſanna's to
the ſon of David:* but woe is me, I am forced
to *hang my harp upon the willows. My feaſt is
turned into mourning, and my ſongs unto lamen-
tation, and the end thereof as a bitter day.*
[Amos viii. 10.] My mind was dark, my
heart hard, my thoughts confuſed, my affections diſordered, my ſoul and all within me
utterly out of frame; I could neither believe,
nor repent, nor hope, nor love, nor do any
thing as I ought to do. I tried and ſtruggled
with myſelf in vain. I was as it were fettered,
pinioned and becalmed, and my very heart
aſleep. In the mean time *my enemies* were
lively; [Pſal. xxxviii. 19.] the devil buſy, and
the world importunate; yea, ten thouſand
trifles amuſing and diſtracting me.

O wretched

O wretched man that I am! [Rom. vii. 24.] When I fhould have been beſt, I was worſt! *When I would do good, evil is preſent with me!* [Ver. 21.] I even tremble to think what a gueſt I was at that holy table; and cannot but wonder that the maſter of the feaſt did not ſingle me out, and ſay, *Friend, how cameſt thou hither?* that he did not ſay to his *ſervants, Bind him hand and foot, and take him away, and caſt him into outer darkneſs.* [Mat. xxii. 12, 13.] I am amazed at the patience of God, that he could bear with ſuch trifling, and did not awaken my drowſy ſoul by ſome terrible judgment; that, ſeeing the *threatning* affected me no more, he did not try what the *execution* would do, according to that of the apoſtle; *for this cauſe many are weak and ſickly among you, and many ſleep.* [1 Cor. ix. 30.]

I adore the divine patience, and will not deſpair of forgiveneſs through the blood of *Jeſus:* But I cannot *forgive* myſelf; and am even out of all *patience,* when I conſider how ſtupid I have been, and how unaccountably I have managed. I could wiſh the ſevereſt providence had detained me; that any thing, *but ſin,* had prevented me from profaning ſuch an ordinance, contracting ſo much guilt, incurring ſuch danger, and creating myſelf ſo much ſorrow.—But alas! 'tis *in vain,* and perhaps *unlawful* ſo to wiſh.

Come then, O my ſoul, inſtead of ſpending time in fruitleſs lamentations, conſider

ſeriouſly what the preſent circumſtance makes
thy duty. Humble thyſelf deeply before
GOD, and *intreat his favour :* ſee if there be
any ground of comfort, and labour to improve ſo ſad a diſappointment (if poſſible) to
ſome good purpoſe.

   ' *God be merciful to me a ſinner !* I acknow-
' ledge my iniquity, and deſire to take to
' myſelf that ſhame which is my due: *Againſt*
' *thee,* O Lord, *have I ſinned,* and thou muſt
' *be juſtified when thou ſpeakeſt, and be clear*
' *when thou judgeſt.* [Pſal. li. 4.] There was
' nothing wanting on thy part; *all things*
' were *ready :* [Mat. xxii. 4] I found a ta-
' ble ſpread, and a cup flowing. The *miniſter*
' performed his part faithfully and devoutly ;
' and it was *only my own* fault that it was
' not a ſweet and edifying ordinance to me,
' as well as others. It was my own ſloth, or
' pride, or unbelief, ſomething or other in
' myſelf, that provoked thy ſpirit to with-
' draw, and cauſed thee to deny that grace,
' without which I can do nothing. I humbly
' confeſs, and heartily lament my walking
' unſuitably to the vows I formerly made,
' and the favours which I have heretofore
' received. I have at this table *ſworn* and
' not *performed,* had *peace ſpoken,* and yet
' *returned again to folly ;* enjoyed ſweet com-
' munion with thee, and yet forgotten, ne-
' glected, and provoked thee. and therefore
' I was juſtly puniſhed, in my *beloved's with-*

' *drawing*

‘ *drawing himself*; so that *when I sought him,*
‘ *I could not find him,* and when *I called him,*
‘ *he gave me no answer:* [Sol. Song, v. 6]
‘ I will therefore *ascribe righteousness to my*
‘ *Maker,* I will *abhor myself, and repent in dust*
‘ *and ashes.* Lord, forgive me, that my pre-
‘ parations were so slight, my self-examina-
‘ tion so superficial, my meditations so loose,
‘ my prayers so cold, and my pains in the
‘ whole so little : pardon me if I omitted
‘ *preparatory* duties, or laid too great stress
‘ upon them ; if *sloth* prevailed with me to
‘ neglect them, or *pride* to trust in them :
‘ forgive me, if by eagerness in worldly bu-
‘ siness, excessive indulgence of the flesh,
‘ in meat or drink, sleep, or needless recrea-
‘ tions, by intemperate passion, or imprudent
‘ ordering of affairs, I not only *provoked* my
‘ GOD, but actually *indisposed myself* for the
‘ holy solemnity : or, if I have been guilty
‘ of any sin, that I ha’n’t duly repented of ;
‘ if I live in the neglect of any known duty,
‘ or under the power of any unmortified lust ;
‘ *shew me,* I beseech thee, *wherefore thou con-*
‘ *tendest with me* ; humble me deeply, wash
‘ me thoroughly, and pardon me freely, for
‘ Jesus sake. *Amen.* ’

But, O my soul, though there be so great
reason for humiliation and self-abasement, I
must not be utterly discouraged, nor *refuse to
be comforted.*

I must hope, that my *heart* has been *right*
with

with GOD, and that I have not wilfully pre-
varicated and trifled with him; therefore
several circumstances may be considered, to
check my *fears* and mitigate my *sorrows*.

I do not serve a *hard master*: a kind and
gracious GOD can make *allowances* for that
indisposition, which may arise from melan-
choly, or other bodily disorders; from extraordinary afflictions, violent temptations,
&c. He *considers our frame*, and knows that
we are but dust, and does not expect the same
from frail *mortals* as he does from the *Angels*
in heaven, and the *spirits of just men made
perfect*. That kind expression of my Lord,
the spirit indeed is willing, but the flesh is weak,
[Matt. xxvi. 41.] may be used to comfort
real and humble christians, though it be often
abused to harden the slothful and presumptu-
ous formalist.]

Let me also consider, that I must not
always conclude an *ordinance lost*, where the
affections have *not been raised*. There may
be *real communion* with GOD, where there is
not a *sensible delight*: the *sacrament* may be
blessed to promote humility and real holiness;
though I have wanted sensible meltings, and
desired manifestations; yea, it is very possible these may be with-held on a wise design,
to carry on the work of GOD in my own soul,
which seems to require a variety of dispensations; as wind and rain, frost and darkness,
are in their proper courses equally necessary

to

to the earth, as calm and fun-fhine. Hereby, it may be, GOD is teaching me *to live more by faith*, upon the righteoufnefs and fulnefs of Jefus; to diftruft *myfelf* more, and cenfure *others* lefs, to be more *watchful, humble, charitable*, and *compaffionate* than ever. I may fee caufe to blefs GOD hereafter for what is fo grievous now. I fhall never forget that faying of my *Lord* to *Peter*, ' *What I do thou* ' *knoweft not now, but thou fhalt know.*' [John xiii. 7]

Befides I would remember that I *cannot prefently judge* of the *benefit* of an *ordinance.* That which is *fown in tears* may be *reaped with joy*; though at prefent there be but fmall appearance of it the fpiritual medicine may gradually mend my conftitution, though it don't operate fenfibly, or prove an immediate cure.

However, I have been doing my *duty*, and GOD may accept my *honeft intentions*; though he don't at prefent fmile upon me and fay, ' *Well done, good and faithful fervant.*'

And, after all, 'tis fome comfort to think that *others have performed more acceptably*, and met with *joy and peace in believing.* And I thank GOD for this fign of grace, that I can rejoice in others being *better* and *more favoured* than myfelf.

But be things as bad as a guilty confci-ence, and an accufing enemy reprefents them; I will blefs GOD, that I have had

grace

grace to *bemoan* myself, lament my folly, and cry to God for mercy, thro' that blood which can atone even for the heinous sin of having interpretatively *counted it an unholy thing.*

And now it remains, that I resolve seriously, in a better strength than my own, to manage better for the time to come. And till an opportunity offers to make a fresh effort, let me walk humbly under a deep sense of my sin, let me be more strict and circumspect in my whole conversation, and live every day under the awe of those *vows of God* which *are upon me.* In an especial manner let me be careful to *keep myself from mine iniquity* [Psal. xviii. 23.] *that* sin to which by my constitution, business, &c. I am most inclined, and with which I am most frequently *overtaken.* Let me be peculiarly careful to perform *those* duties to which I find a corrupt heart most averse. This will be the best way to retrieve the loss I have sustained. God forbid that I should encourage myself in future neglects, by any considerations whatfoever: yet I must believe that *he* remembers Christ in the Sacrament to the *best purpose, who,* under the sense of what he has there professed and promised, *lives best* after it, being well assured that a holy conversation, upon *gospel* principles and motives, is a better evidence of worthy receiving, than all the transports and ecstasies imaginable. I would not be satisfied without being *affected*; but

surely

Surely the *principal* thing is by so apt a means to be *improved* and *bettered*; *to grow in grace and in the knowledge of our Lord and Saviour Jesus Christ.* [2 Pet. iii. 18.]

Therefore I must make it my earnest and daily prayer, that GOD would *bless* his ordinance to this great end; or else my labour will be lost, and my expectations frustrate.

And Oh! that he would vouchsafe his blessing accordingly! grant, that I may never forget the engagements I am under; but upon every occasion remember that I *am a Christian,* and have solemnly owned *Christ;* that this thought may be a restraint from *sin,* and a spur to *duty;* an antidote against all the poisonous *suggestions* of the grand enemy of souls, a preservative from the *ill examples* of those *children of disobedience, in whom he works,* [Eph. ii. 2.] and a cordial under all the *troubles* and *afflictions* of this mortal life. May I find so great benefit by thus waiting upon GOD, that I may long for the return of such seasons; and by *frequent communion* with saints on earth, be fitted for better company in a better world; when I shall *sit down with Abraham, Isaac and Jacob, in the kingdom of God;* yea, *be with Christ where he is, and behold his glory;* which is *all my salvation, and all my desire.* Amen.

End of the First Part.

PART II.

The Chriſtian's *Conduct* after *the Sacrament of the* Lord's Supper, *directed, &c.*

The INTRODUCTION.

THAT the ſacrament of the LORD's *Supper* is a ſtanding ordinance in the chriſtian church, I ſhall now take for granted; my concern not being at preſent with *ſuch*, as call it *in queſtion*. I am applying myſelf to *thoſe*, who have, with conſcience towards GOD, attended upon the ſolemnity, and are deſirous that all the great ends of it may be anſwered; the ſum of which is the *honour of* GOD, and the *edification of our own ſouls*. This is what every *ſerious perſon* propoſes *before* his actual participation, and is obliged to purſue *after* it.

Of *preparatory* duties *many* have written; and I have thrown *my* mite into the *common* treaſury. Of a proper behaviour *after* the ſacrament, I would ſay ſomething by itſelf: not as tho' it were a ſubject *untouched*; but as it may be conſidered without ſo much *inter-ferïng* with the performances of others; it

D 4   not

not having been fo *profeffedly* and *diftinctly*
treated of, as thofe previous difpofitions,
which ought to be made in order to our being worthy communicants. And befides, I
engage in this fervice with a particular view,
hoping to make an advantageous reprefentation of this plain and important truth ; *that
the right improvement of* one *communion, is the
beft preparation for* another.

Partaking of the *Lord's Supper* is one of
thofe, which *divines* call *inftrumental* duties;
fuch are all parts of external worfhip.—Not
that they are *merely* fo ; for they are defigned
to exprefs our duty to GOD, and in them we
pay a homage to our fupreme Lord So in
eating and *drinking* the confecrated elements,
we *remember Chrift,* and *fhew forth his death,*
and therein do homage to him who is exalted and made Lord of all : we confefs that
Jefus is Lord, to the glory of GOD *the Father.*
[Phil. ii 11.]—Nor are they, properly fpeak-
ing, *principally* fo , for, tho' in our *chief* end,
complexly confidered, the *glory of* GOD and
our own falvation, are *infeparable ;* yet the *former* is in ftrict propriety our *ultimate end,*
and what is of *prior* confideration to the other
—But they are *truly* fo, being defigned as
means to anfwer this great end, that we may
be *made meet to be partakers of the inheritance
of the faints in light.* [Colof i. 12] Particularly the Lord's Supper is, by all forts of
chriftian

christian writers, represented as conducing to this end. *Worthy receivers are by faith made partakers of Christ's body and blood to their spiritual nourishment and growth in grace*, says one Catechism, [Assembly's ·] *our souls are strengthened and refreshed by the body and blood of Christ, as our bodies are by bread and wine*, says another, [Church of *England*]

Now that this end may be answered, we must take diligent heed to ourselves after the solemnity is *over*, as well as prepare carefully *before*, and attend closely *at* the administration For, consider,

1 The sacrament does not operate after the manner of an *amulet*, or *charm*, which are said to effect cures or preserve from dangers by the mere external application; and *that* even in the case of infants and idiots, who know nothing of the matter —nor in a *natural* way; as medicines rightly prepared and administered do really heal diseases, whether there be any attention of mind to the operation or not. The effect of *sacraments* is not *ex opero operato*, (as the popish schoolmen barbarously express an absurd or unintelligible notion) No man can be so weak as to suppose that the soul can receive any moral benefit from the mere eating of bread and wine; for they are (as Mr. *Vines* observes, p. 41) *incommensurate and improper to the soul; and the body may be more easily fed with air, than the soul with bread and wine.*

D 5

Nay,

Nay, if we allow the elements to be *turned into*, or *contain under* them the real body and blood of Chrift ; for that is the fenfe (or meaning at leaft) of thofe two hard words *Tranfubftantiation* and *Confubftantiation*, which (as the forementioned author obferves, p. 8) have *bred more jars, and coft more blood, fince they were born (and neither of them are fix hundred years old) than can be well imagined*. I fay, if the bread and wine were in a *corporal* manner Chrift's flefh and blood, the mere taking them into the body could not anfwer any fpiritual faving purpofes : for thus our Saviour himfelf fays, *The flefh profiteth nothing*. [John vi. 63. Vid. *Whitby* ad loc]

2. The operation of the facrament is by way of *moral* inftrumentality. It is a means *appointed* by GOD for our *edification*, and apparently *fit* and *proper* for that purpofe Under whatever view we confider it, as a memorial, an expreffion of gratitude, an obligation, oath, or vow; it has a tendency to promote the divine life, and is to be improved accordingly ; and the fuccefs depends upon our attending to it, with ferious and diligent application, under the influences of GOD's holy fpirit, whofe bleffing may be expected upon his own inftitutions.   And,

3. Therefore, after the tranfaction is over, we muft take heed to ourfelves, left we *lofe the*

the things which we have wrought. We are not to suppose, that having devoutly received the elements (how strong soever our faith and hope and love were at that time) our concern is over, when the ordinance is ended. 'Tis true, some ends are answered as soon as the ceremony is finished, *viz.* the solemn renewing of our baptismal covenant, the open profession of Christ, or shewing forth his death, and every thing that may be called *doing our homage* (as far as it is so;) these ends, I say, are answered by worthy receivers, before they return from the solemnity. But as it is an *instrumental* duty, they have then only laid a fresh foundation for further work, by putting themselves under strong engagements and receiving great encouragements; and their after-business must be to build a superstructure of holiness and comfort.

CHAP. I.

Of reviewing *our* Behaviour *at the* Ordinance.

IN order to the *ends* of the sacrament being answered in our advancing in goodness; or, in the apostle's words, *growing in grace, and in the knowledge of our Lord and Saviour Jesus Christ,* [2 Pet. iii. 18.] it appears requisite, that we should take the first proper

op-

opportunity to review our behaviour. It is our duty to *examine* ourselves *before* the participation, if we would be worthy *receivers*; and *after* it, if we would *walk* worthily. It may be proper to call ourselves to account, whether we allowed such a proportion of time, as our circumstances would admit, to search our hearts, and try our ways, to humble our souls, and confess our sins, and cry for mercy; to strengthen our faith, confirm our hope, and inflame our love to God and Christ, and one another; to form resolutions, to settle rules for our future conduct, &c. and whether the time we separated to these purposes was faithfully employed according to the design; and what the issue of it was; whether we went forth to the house of God with a seriousness of spirit, and had our minds impressed with such thoughts as were proper for the occasion.

But especially, we should recollect the manner of our behaviour at the solemnity; whether an awe of God fell upon us, when we addressed ourselves to the service: at least, whether we endeavoured to *set the Lord before us*, and considered, that *all things are naked and opened unto the eyes of him with whom we have to do*; [Heb. iv. 13] that the secrets of our *hearts* are as full in his view, as the air of our *countenances*; and the temper of our
mind

mind as much within his obfervation, as the pofture of our *bodies*: that the omniprefent, omnifcient GOD is alfo a jealous one; and that, as he *cannot* be deceived, he *will not* be mocked; as he cannot be impofed upon, he will not be trifled with, that he requires the heart, and will accept of nothing without it; and that nothing external, how laborious or expenfive foever, fhall be admitted as equivalent to a ferious devotion of fpirit · that humble geftures, covered faces, uplifted eyes, heaving breafts, and forced tears, are nothing (or worfe) without that *inward* temper, which they are defigned to exprefs.

Whether we left the world behind us, when we went up to worfhip; at leaft endeavoured to bar our hearts againft the intrufion of every thing foreign and impertinent to the purpofe before us; efpecially guarding against finful imaginations, and the workings of a vain, proud, fenfual, covetous, and revengeful fpirit.

Whether we had our hearts in fome good meafure fixed and attentive to the important bufinefs we were engaged in; and fet ourfelves to check their unfeafonable wandrings and improper excurfions. If we did (in the old *facrifical* phrafe) *hoc agere*, mind what we were about; or, according to the ecclefiaftical *formula*, *furfum corda*, lift up our hearts in the fervice.

Whether

Whether we were suitably affected with what we saw and heard, and were duly impressed with the various thoughts which passed through our minds. Whether our *faith* was in vigorous exercise, and we found ourselves firmly persuaded of the truth of those things, which were represented or shewed forth to us in the *ordinance*; particularly, that *Christ died for our sins, according to the scriptures*, [1 Cor. xv. 3.] shewing forth Christ's death being one great end of the institution. Whether while we *mused, the fire burned*: If our hearts *burned within us*, while we beheld the memorial of his broken body, and the representation of *that* blood, which was shed for the remission of our sins. If it excited our love to him, when we beheld how he loved us. Whether we mourned over him whom our sins had pierced; loathed ourselves for our abominations; wished we had been suffering any thing, rather than sinning against God; and resolved by his grace, that we would be at an eternal defiance with that accursed thing which created this tragedy. Whether we heartily *accepted* Christ to the ends for which God exalted him, namely, *to be a prince and a saviour, to give repentance and forgiveness of sins*, [Acts v. 31.] and vowed in a better strength than our own, that we would follow him wherever he should lead us, and go wherever he should send

fend us. Whether we heartily *resigned* ourfelves to the conduct of divine providence,
protesting that we would take every thing
kindly, which our Lord should order as to
our circumstances in life; and be ready to
die and go hence when he should call us;
and that in the mean time our whole *spirit*,
foul and *body*, all our powers, poffeffions and
interefts, to the utmoft extent of our influence, should be at his fervice, and devoted
to his glory. Whether we entertained a
comfortable *hope* of mercy, and could in any
good meafure rejoice in the hope of the glory
of God. In a word, whether we experienced
the workings of *gratitude* to God for his in-
eftimable love; and of a right and *charitable*
fpirit towards even ftrangers and enemies,
but efpecially towards all the *houfhold of faith*,
wherever fcattered, and however diftinguifh-
ed; all fuch, of what party or denomination
foever, as *love our Lord Jefus Chrift in fincerity*; [Eph. vi. 24] and fo have an intereft
in the common falvation. [Jude ver. 3.]

CHAP. II.

Concerning our Duty ; *if upon examination we find, our* Attendance *has been, in the main,* regular.

IF by God's bleffing we find reafon to conclude, that our *behaviour* has been *right*, and our *conduct* fuch, as a well in-ftructed confcience approves, in the general, and with proper allowances, our *duty* appears to be as follows.

1. We muft *blefs* God. Surely chriftians need not be reafoned with to make them fen-fible, that *every good gift, and every perfect gift is* from God ; [James i. 17.] and that he *worketh in us both to will and to do :* [Philip. ii. 13.] that it is true as to the *fpiritual*, as well as *natural life*, that *in him we live and move*, and *his are all our ways* The *habits* of grace are from him, and the *exercife* of them are under his direction and influence. This we *confefs* in our *prayers*, and fhould alfo *own* in our *praifes :* for nothing can be more unaccountable than to expect from God, and afcribe to felf. If he gave the holy fpirit at our afking, is he not to be praifed by fuch as receive it ? He has not been under the influences of the di-vine fpirit at the Lord's table, who is not ready to fay, *Bleffed be God, even the Father*

of

of our Lord *Jesus Christ, who hath blessed us with spiritual blessings,* &c. [Eph. i. 3.] He, whose *heart* has been *fixed,* will *sing and give praise.* The words of *David,* upon another solemn occasion, are very proper upon this: *Now, therefore, our God, we thank thee, and praise thy glorious name. But who am I, and what is my people, that we should be able to offer so willingly after this sort?* [1 Chr. xxix. 13, 14]

To *quicken* our *thankfulness,* we may do well to call to mind, if it have not often been otherwise with us; such of us especially as have been *communicants* many years, who have *been* long *planted in the house of the Lord,* and appeared to *flourish in the courts of our God,* may well remember the different seasons which have passed over us. We have oftentimes been disappointed in our expectations. We have gone out full of hopes, and returned empty of comfort, and have had reason to apply to ourselves in a spiritual sense that of the prophet; *they returned with their vessels empty, they were ashamed and covered their heads.* [Jer. xiv. 3.]

Thro' the prevalence of an *evil heart* of unbelief, the importunate solicitations of the *world,* and the suggestions of our indefatigable *adversary,* has it not often happened to us, *as when a hungry man dreameth, and behold he eateth; but he awaketh, and his soul is empty?* or, *as when a thirsty man dreameth,*

and

and behold he drinketh; but he awaketh, and behold he is faint, and his soul hath appetite [Isa. xxix. 8] The *bread* we expected has been as a *stone*; our *wine* mixed with *water*; yea, that which should have been a *cup of blessing*, has been like that which they offered our Saviour, and he would not drink, *vinegar mingled with gall* [Matt. xxvii. 34.] This thought should warm our hearts into thankful acknowledgments, if we *have sat under his shadow with great delight, and his fruit has been sweet to our taste* : if we have *tasted and seen that the Lord is gracious* : if in the holy ordinance, GOD has remembered us, with *the love which he bears to his own, and visited us with his salvation*. In a word, we should conclude our *review*, as we did the *solemnity* itself, with a hymn of praise, an hallelujah, in such words as the psalmist uses; *Bless the Lord, O my soul, and all that is within me bless his holy name. bless the Lord, O my soul, and forget not all his benefits.* [Psal. cui. ad init.]

2. We must pray and endeavour, that the *impressions* we have received may *abide*; that they may not be *as the morning-cloud and early dew*, which goeth away, like a small shower, which sprinkleth the thirsty earth, and drying away in a little while, leaves the grass more parched than it was before. Such a request *David* added to his thanksgivings aforementioned; *O Lord, keep this for ever in the*
imagi-

imagination of the thoughts of the heart of thy people, and prepare (or, as it is in the margin, and may properly be read, *stablish*) *their hearts unto thee.* [1 Chr. xxix. 18] We should earnestly beseech God, that we may bear in mind what passed at the awful solemnity, that what we saw, and felt, and heard, and vowed, may not be forgotten, or remembred as waters that pass away, but may possess our souls, and be as *nails fastened by the masters of assemblies:* [Eccles. xii. 11.] that as God *satisfied our mouth with good things,* when he made unto his people *a feast of fat things, a feast of wine on the lees, of fat things full of marrow, of wine on the lees well refined,* [Isai. xxv. 6.] we may not soon lose the relish of those royal dainties, which his table yielded. The murmuring *Israelites* could long retain the savour of the *fleshpots of* Egypt, and remembered *the fish they did eat in* Egypt *freely, the cucumbers and melons, and the leeks and the onions and the garlick;* [Numb. xi. 5.] and shall not the *Israel* of God, the true circumcision, remember the heavenly manna they tasted at that table which he spread for them in the wilderness? Let us not easily forget with what peculiar satisfaction we fed on him, whose *flesh is meat indeed, and whose blood is drink indeed:* for this purpose let us *bow our knees to the Father of our Lord Jesus Christ.* [Eph. iii. 14.]

And

' And to our prayers we muſt join anſwer-able *endeavours*, otherwiſe we mock GOD, and deceive ourſelves: we muſt *guard* againſt every thing which tends to wear off the im-preſſions we have received, or leſſen their force. Whatever care we take (ſuch is the frailty of our nature) the glory which we ſaw, and the ſweetneſs which we taſted, while the *king ſat at his table*, will abate in a very great proportion: and for this reaſon GOD has mercifully provided for the renew-ing of our agreeable and uſeful ſenſations, by the frequent return of the day of our feſtival ſolemnities: however, it concerns us to watch againſt every thing that may ob-literate the impreſſions, which the ſight of a *crucified* Jeſus, and the believing views of a *glorified* and *ſhortly to be revealed one*, left upon us.

Particularly, we muſt watch againſt every *wilful ſin*: this is of principal importance in the caſe. Any one wilful, eſpecially groſs ſin, will efface the deepeſt and ſtrongeſt impreſ-ſions, which the ordinance has made: the caſe will be, as when a man has been taking a great deal of pains to kindle ill-diſpoſed materials into a flame, and then throws water upon it when he has done; his labour is loſt, and the work grows more difficult. By wil-ful ſin the *ſpirit* is *quenched,* [1 Theſ. v. 19] i. e. as to his operations, in the ſame manner,

ner, as he is faid to be *grieved*. [Eph. iv. 30.]
Upon this account *David*, after he had committed thofe aggravated abominations of
murder and adultery, had a great deal of
reafon to pray, *Take not thy holy fpirit from
me:* [Pfal. li. 11.] and crimes of a great
deal *lighter dye* will in their proportion have
the fame effect, efpecially if they are committed not only againft full light and certain
knowledge, but againft the actual remon-
ftrances of a faithful confcience. Or, if matters do not go that *dreadful* length, (as it may
be hoped they feldom do) yet, if for want of
watchfulnefs and fobriety of mind we are
overtaken with any groffer fault, the confequence will be very unhappy, and we may
expect damage as to peace or tendernefs of
our confcience, and that, inftead of that
difpofition to communion with God, which
we brought away from the regularly attended
ordinance, there will arife a fort of fhynefs
and eftrangement betwixt us and him whom
our fouls love. We fhall lofe our *confidence
towards* God, and he will hide his face from
us: ' *He* will act *towards us*, as men are
' wont to do, when they are grieved by us,
' and difpleafed at us, withdrawing their
' wonted kindnefs, flying our company, and
' abandoning us to our enemies:' [*V.* Whitby in Eph. iv. 30.] and *we* fhall be apt to
carry *towards him*, as we are ufed to do unto
a friend, whom we have injurioufly treated,
and

and inexcufably affronted, fhun his prefence, and avoid his converfation.

We ought alfo to watch againft an *inordinate* attention to the things of this *world*. Circumftances at prefent will not allow us always to dwell in GOD's houfe; after a fhort ftay we muft come down from the mount, and our delightful converfe with GOD muft be interrupted by the moderate cares, bufinefs, and diverfions of life: but if we would not *lofe the things which we have wrought*, we muft fee that our regard to common affairs be kept within the bounds of moderation. Carking *cares* will four and contract our minds, and *eat as doth a canker*: multiplicity of *bufinefs* (when we are not clearly obliged to it) will diftract us, and hinder thofe reflections, which muft at proper intervals be made ufe of, as means to keep alive the holy flame, which our mufings kindled at the bleffed folemnity: while we are careful about many things, it will be hard to do any thing well, and it is odds but the *one thing needful* will be the moft neglected. The fame or greater need there is, that we fet proper bounds to the *diverfions* and amufements of life. Exceffive mirth, protracted feafts, and exorbitant play will carnalize our frame, and by habitual indulgence produce the fame effect, as things in themfelves more criminal; and in fome refpects are more dangerous, as they fteal upon us infenfibly,

fibly, and are not fo fhocking in the review as more flagrant crimes are; into which alfo they too often lead us, ere we are aware. Nay, the *amufements of learning* itfelf, how refined and abftracted foever they are, if purfued with too much eagernefs, and without due reft and paufes, may rob us of our treafure, and as effectually put us out of the temper we ought to maintain, as even fenfual excesses themfelves. I appeal for the truth of this, not only to fuch as delight in mathematicks, hiftory, and poetry, but even thofe who are engaged in controverfial ftudies, though the fubject be divine, and the fpeculation moft fublime. All thefe things, if inordinately profecuted, come within the reach of that prohibition, *love not the world, nether the things that are in the world: if any man love the world, the love of the Father is not in him.* [1 John ii 15.]

We muft alfo be upon our guard againft excefs of *worldly forrow*. of this the apoftle faith, that it *worketh death* [2 Cor. vii. 10.] The expreffion is, no doubt, to be underftood of death in the *literal* fenfe: but it is alfo true, that an inordinate indulgence to it is very prejudicial to the intereft of the *divine life* in the foul: this forrow evidently proceeds from too great a fondnefs for temporal things; and as evidently tends to abate the fenfe and relifh of divine things, which ought to be be preserved upon the mind; and for the maintaining of which in its proper vigour, we make use of the sacrament of the Lord's supper, as a choice and special means.

I confess, afflictions are designed and suited to do us good, and promote our most valuable interests. *By the sadness of the countenance the heart is made better :* [Eccles. vii. 3.] *whom the Lord loveth he chasteneth, and it is for our profit, that we may be partakers of his holiness; and it yieldeth the peaceable fruits of righteousness to them that are exercised thereby :* [Heb. xii. 6, 10, 11.] and it is acknowledged that a degree of sorrow, when we are under the corrections of our heavenly father, is natural and very becoming his children : but still there may be an excess, which is a fault, and produces ill effects; particularly *this,* that it abates the spirituality of our temper, which is the desired and agreeable result of our well-regulated devotions. Men may prejudice themselves by carrying their worldly sorrows too high, as well as by intemperance in their joys. As our *prosperity* hurts us, when it dilates the heart unreasonably; so does our *adversity,* when it sinks us beyond measure. Affliction never has its kindly effect, but when we are in a meek, resigned, and heavenly frame, to which such degrees of worldly sorrow, as I have been cautioning against, are by no means friendly.

3. If

3. If our attendance upon the ordinance hath been well managed, and produced the prefent defired effect, it is fit we fhould confider very ferioufly, that we ought not to lay too *great a ftrefs* upon the *good frame* we find ourfelves in. This may prove a fnare to us. for though it be a very defirable thing to have our hearts warmed, and our affections raifed by the fteady contemplation of divine things, when they are offered to our minds under an advantageous reprefentation ; yet we muft not reft in this, as if all the ends of communicating were anfwered. The reafon of this appears from what has been hinted before, concerning the facrament's being an *inftrumental* duty. It is defigned to help us in the more proper and effectual difcharge of all thofe things, to which the profeffion of chriftianity obligeth us and it is obvious to any common underftanding, that fitting ourfelves for our work, is a diftinct thing from the actual performing of it. This *fpiritual repaft* is defigned to ftrengthen us for the way and work which are before us, and we all know, that tho' our food be ever fo good, and we eat it with ever fo much pleafure, and feel the cheering and ftrengthening effects of it in the beft manner one would wifh ; yet if in the ftrength of it we do not go forward in our journey, or apply diligently to our bufinefs, we are far from anfwering the end of our refrefhments : yea, our loitering and neglect

. E of

of bufinefs is by this means an offence of greater aggravation.—Therefore,

4. We muft be fure to *improve* all the fpiritual refrefhment we got at the Lord's table to the *great purpofes of life.* The end, which every man ought to propofe in living, and which at this facrament we openly engage ourfelves to purfue, is to glorify and pleafe the great God, by doing his will, and fo to work out our own falvation · let every communicant therefore be duly apprized, that whatever emotions he may feel at the ordinance, his labour is loft, and in fome refpects worfe than loft, if the intereft of inward holinefs and practical godlinefs be not ferved by it our coming together is not for the better, if it do not make us fo and that, both in the temper of our mind, and the courfe of our converfation.

(1.) In the *temper* of our *mind.* The end of *all ordinances*, and particularly of *this* moft folemn one, is to make the heart better. While men are abfolutely in an unregenerate ftate, the inward part, the hidden man, is altogether overfpread with darknefs, covered with confufion, and in a moft wild diforder : their reafon either lies afleep, or is mifled by falfe appearances and unhappy prejudices · their paffions are ftrong and turbulent, and their cafe is aptly defcribed by the prophet under the metaphor of a *troubled fea when it cannot reft, whofe waters caft up mire and dirt.* [Ifa. lvii. 20.]
The

The ſpirit of God makes a *change* in thoſe who are *born again*; a change which is indeed happy and amazing , they are in a good meaſure the reverſe of what they were , reaſon reſumes its empire, and the tumultuous paſſions ſubſide, they come to themſelves, and are in a right mind after a ſad ſtate of diſtraction ; they think right and project well, and behave with a viſible ſobriety. This change is expreſſed by a great variety of *metaphors* in ſcripture, which ſtrike every attentive mind ſo ſtrongly, that they are eaſily recollected: but ſtill the good work is *only begun*, when we are *firſt* born of God ; it muſt be *carried on* gradually to perfection We are compared to *new-born babes*, and are to attend the *word* (under which goſpel ordinances are comprehended) *that we may grow thereby*: [1 Pet ii. 2] *till we come to a perfect man, to the meaſure of the ſtature of the fulneſs of Chriſt*. [Eph. iv. 13.] We muſt therefore conſider ſeriouſly that the end of our taking this ſpiritual nouriſhment is our growth in grace

We are not to be ſatisfied, how well ſoever we ſeem to perform at the holy ſolemnity, unleſs we find a growing conformity to Chriſt our head; that we become more like him, and have more of that *mind in us which was in Chriſt Jeſus*, [Philip. ii. 5.] this is meant by *putting on the Lord Jeſus Chriſt*, as it ſtands oppoſed to *making proviſion for the fleſh, to*

ſulfil

fulfil *the lusts* thereof: [Rom. xiii. 14.] this is *putting on the new man, which after God is created in righteousness and true holiness.* [Eph. iv. 24] We must, if we would approve ourselves worthy communicants, aim vehemently and press earnestly after that perfection, of which the holy Jesus is the high *exemplar,* or complete pattern. Let the words and example of him, who was so close a follower of Christ, dwell much upon our minds : *Brethren, I count not myself to have apprehended; but this one thing I do, forgetting those things which are behind, and reaching forth unto those things which are before, I press towards the mark,* &c [Philip. iii. 13, 14] To this purpose I shall apply those words of the same apostle ; *having these promises* (which are represented, sealed, and applied to believers in the Lord's supper) *let us cleanse ourselves from all filthiness both of flesh and spirit, perfecting holiness in the fear of the Lord* [2 Cor. vii. 1.] Let us see that our *faith grow exceedingly,* and that, by the help of such apt means, that which is *lacking in it be perfected,* that we be *strong in faith, giving glory to God;* that we *abound in hope thro' the power of the Holy Ghost* ; that we make a discernible progress in that *more excellent* way of *charity,* which is the spring and sum of all our duty both towards God and man ; that we advance in *purity* of heart, in opposition to all sensual defilements, and those *fleshly lusts,*
which

which war against the soul; that *patience have
its perfect work*, which is a branch of that
humility, which is of the greatest consequence
to secure his favour, who has told us, that
he *resists the proud, and gives grace to the humble* [James iv 6] in a word, that we *grow
up into him in all things, who is the head, even
Christ*. [Eph. iv. 15.]

(2.) In the course of our *conversation*;
this is the proof of the former, as the *effect*
is of the *cause* a better *life* is a proper evidence of a better *heart*. This therefore we
must see to, that in our whole conduct *our
profiting* by the holy ordinance *may* abundantly *appear* :—that we may be more strictly
just, and more diffusively *good* (in that sense
in which the apostle uses the word; *perad-
venture for a good man one would even dare to
die* .) [Rom. v 7.] —that as we profess to
bear Christ's *image*, and improve in it, we
follow his *example* more exactly, who *went
about doing good* , so far, that our zeal may
provoke others :—that we be more *meek* and
lowly in our behaviour towards our neighbour,
and appear more remarkably in the ornament
of a *quiet* spirit .—that we be better in every
relation, and fill up the place, in which providence has set us, with greater exactness and
decorum : — that we be better husbands,
wives, parents, children, magistrates, mini-
sters, masters, servants, &c.—that we shew
a greater government over our appetites,

E 3 passions,

paffions, and tongues, and in the comprehenfive words of the apoftle, live more *foberly,
righteoufly, and godly in this prefent world*.
[Tit. ii 12.]—that we fhew forth the effect
this appointed means has on us, by our being
purged, fo as to *bring forth more fruit*; [John
xv 2] and *being filled with the fruits of
righteoufnefs, which are by Chrift Jefus to the
praife and glory of God*: [Philip. i. 11.] in a
word, that *as we have received, how we ought
to walk, and to pleafe* God, *we may abound
more and more*. [1 Theff. iv. 1.] This is that
ordering the converfation aright, to which the
promi'e is made of *feeing the falvation of* God:
[Pfal. l. 2g.] that work of the Lord, in
which if we always *abound*, our *labour fhall
not be in vain in the Lord* [1 Cor. xv ult]

I have hinted already, that it is fit that it
be diftinctly reprefented, that *to all this* we
oblige ourfelves at the Lord's table in the moft
folemn manner · we then bind our fouls with
an *oath*, and come under a vow, to do our
utmoft, that we may increafe in holinefs,
and perfevere in it to the end. And need i
prove, that how grave and ferious and affected foever we be *at* the awful ceremony,
the *end* is not anfwered, unlefs we be true to
our oath and folemn engagement ? Let us
remember the words of the wife man, which
are applicable to the prefent purpofe, *when
thou voweft a vow unto God, defer not to pay
it · for he hath no pleafure in fools, pay that
which*

which thou haft vowed. [Ecclef. v. 4.] The representation, which is made of Chrift's body and blood in the *facrament*, is defigned to draw forth our hatred againft fin, under the imputation of which he fuffered, and to excite us to effectual purpofes againft it, and at the fame time to engage our refolutions to exprefs our love to him, who *loved us, and gave himfelf for us*, in doing whatfoever he commands us. *This* we acknowledge to be our *reafonable* fervice; *this* we purpofe, promife and vow, when we feaft upon the memorials of his facrifice, and *this* we muft perform, or elfe we *give the facrifice of fools*. [Ecclef. v. 1.]

Let it be alfo confidered, that as we lay ourfelves under obligations, fo we profefs our *expectation* of Goɒ's *fpirit and grace* to help us, that this great end may be attained; and indeed our expectations are well grounded, even upon a fure word of promife, that *our heavenly father will give the holy fpirit to them that afk him*. [Luke xi. 13.] now moft certainly a promife of affiftance inforces an obligation. If Goɒ has appointed the *ordinance*, as a *means* to this *end*, and has promifed his *grace*, if duly applied to, for the *effecting* it, furely we are obliged to purfue it with all poffible application and perfeverance. Thus much is plainly declared in that of the apoftle, *work out your own falvation, for it is God that worketh in you both to will and to do*

L 4   *accord-*

according to his good pleasure. [Philip. ii. 12, 13.]

Thus I have shewed what *is* our *duty*, if our *attendance* upon the *sacrament* has been in any good degree *regular* and *comfortable*: what our *conduct must be*, if it has been *otherwise*, falls next under consideration.

C H A P. III.

Shewing what is our Duty, *if our Behaviour at the Lord's Table hath been very irregular or* uncomfortable.

IF upon reflection we find, that we have been more than ordinarily indisposed at the blessed ordinance, if our *faith* has been weak, our *thoughts* distracted, our *hearts* cold, and our *adversary* prevalent; our duty may be represented under the following particulars.

1. Let us be *humbled in our souls before God.* If our disappointment was the effect of bodily indisposition, or some sore affliction in our family, and we forced ourselves to the Lord's table, to shew our regard to the ordinance, and with hope of finding relief; we are even in this case to humble ourselves under the mighty hand of God, and be

duly

duly fenfible of the righteoufnefs of his pro-
ceedings, confeffing that we d ferve every
rebuke he is pleafed to direct: however, *this*
fhould be confidered as *an affliction*, which
we ought to bear with patience; and endeavour to comfort ourfelves, that we have not
to do with a rigorous judge, but a compaffionate father, who *knoweth our frame, and re-
membereth we are duft.*

But I fuppofe confcience juftly charging
our difappointment upon *our mifconduct*:
then we ought to take *fhame* to ourfelves,
and *forrow after a godly fort*, for that floth,
fenfuality, or worldly-mindednefs, which
hindered our regular preparations, or that
pride and felf-conceit which made us lay
too great a a ftrefs upon them, or whatever
corrupt affections hindered our devotion at
the communion, and gave Satan an advantage over us. If we encourage confcience
to be faithful, we fhall, without need of a
divine revelation, be able to find out the
accurfed thing, to which God's withdrawing
himfelf from us is to be imputed; to what
it is owing, that we did not find him whom
our fouls love, nor *fee his power and his glory,
as we have feen it in the fanctuary.* And upon
confideration of the whole matter, as confcience regulated by the word of God fhall
reprefent it, let us be fuitably affected, ab-
horring ourfelves, and expreffing our concern in proper tokens of humiliation; as

E 5 *Ezra*

Ezra (in another cafe) fell upon his knees, and fpread out his hands to the Lord his GOD, and faid, *O my* GOD, *I am afhamed, and blufh to lift up my face to thee my God*; [Ezra ix. 5, 6.] confeffing and bewailing our fins *in general*, and that corruption *particularly*, to which we apprehend our mifmanagement and difappointment is principally owing.

And, if our repentance be fincere and hearty, we have no reafon to doubt of obtaining mercy through *that* blood, which *cleanfeth from all fin*. For this we muft pray earneftly, and to quicken our applications to the throne of grace, let us confider, that no fmall guilt is contracted by our mifbehaviour at the Lord's table. I would watch againft faying any thing to grieve a tender fpirit, and have intimated the allowances GOD will make in cafe of bodily diforder, and lamented infirmities, *&c.* but furely it is no light thing to be *guilty of the body and blood of the Lord*, [1 Cor. xi. 27.] and yet fo they are, who *eat the bread, and drink the cup, unworthily*; fuch are faid to eat and drink *damnation* or judgment *to themfelves*. And how much foever thefe paffages, which found fo terribly, may be foftened by attending to the import of the original words, and fcope of the context, yet no room can be left after all to doubt, that a good man may be very guilty in this matter; and when he ftands
con-

convicted by his own conscience of inexcusable neglect, ought to beg forgiveness
in this case, in the same manner as he uses to
do upon occasion of any of the grosser follies of his life. And tho' I would not intimate it to be the sense of that text, *Heb* x
29. which certainly speaks of final apostasy;
yet a serious mind will not scruple to charge
himself with some share in the guilt of having
trodden under foot the Son of God, and counted
the blood of the covenant, wherewith he was
sanctified, an unholy thing, and done despite to
the spirit of Grace , and will even apply to
his own case that prayer in the penitential
psalm, *Deliver me from blood-guiltiness, O God,*
thou God of my salvation, and my tongue shall
sing aloud of thy righteousness. [Psal. li. 14.]
However, it is certainly fit, that upon such
occasions we should confess our fault, own
our demerit, deprecate the divine displeasure,
and resolve by God's grace to take more
heed for the time to come; that we engage
in awful solemnities with a more suitable
frame of spirit, and decency of *inward* as
well as *outward* behaviour.

2 Let us *use proper methods to retrieve our*
fault, as much as may be, and the damage
we have sustained by unworthy receiving:
and this is to be attempted,

[1.] Not merely by waiting the return
of another opportunity. Indeed, we are
with full purpose of heart to promise, that,

if

if God shall bring us to his table again, we will endeavour to behave better; but this is far from being sufficient. It will not satisfy a well-directed conscience, but leave us under an uneasy regret for having lost a prize which was put into our hands, and that perhaps irretrievably; for as what is passed cannot be recalled, so we may not live to see the dawn of another day of the Son of man, or have another opportunity of rectifying what was amiss in our former management by our future care. But,

[2.] By diligent application to the duties, which are statedly subsequent to a communion. If we have not succeeded as we ought, desired, and expected, the concern about our miscarriage should quicken us to the more care and pains in those duties, which are to be attended to, in pursuance of the great end of communicating, whatever our frame has been at the time of it. The end of this ordinance is certainly our *increase in holiness*, there we see the most powerful *motives* to it, represented in the most moving manner, there we lay ourselves under the strongest *obligations*, and receive the greatest *encouragements*, and our business is to take care, that our conduct be regulated accordingly in the whole of our behaviour towards God and man: the particulars of which are obvious to a willing and

and ſerious mind, and have been repreſented in their proper place.

I ſhall only remark under this head, that though our doubling our diligence in after-duties is not a proper atonement for our culpable neglects at the time of participation, yet it is what we *ought* to do, and is the beſt thing we *can* do; and the wonderful grace of GOD may order the matter ſo, as to bring good out of this evil; and we may hope will do it, if our repentance be expreſſed in more cloſe reflections, ſerious reſolutions, ſtrict watchfulneſs, and earneſt prayers, upon the account of the omiſſions and miſcarriages we bewail. And though no wiſe man would chuſe to ſleep beyond his hour, or ſtumble in his way, 'tis no uncommon thing for after-diligence to retrieve it, and make even the misfortune turn to account.

CHAP. IV.

Recommending the frequent Recollection *of what paſs'd at the Sacrament, in order to our* ſpiritual Improvement.

HITHERTO I have been repreſenting what I apprehend, in the main, (and making proper allowances) to be the com-

communicant's *duty*, in order to the improvement of the life of God in his soul, by the ordinance of the Holy Supper. I come now to propose something merely by way of *advice*; concerning the expediency of which I leave every man, who has a taste of devotion, to determine for himself. What I aim at, is, that we set the solemnity before us in our daily walk or conversation, *after* our first serious recollections and reflections are over. However our management and success appears to have been upon a serious enquiry, it may be proper *daily* to lead back our thoughts to what passed between God and our souls at *the great solemnity:* and this both *statedly* in our retirements for devotion; and *occasionally* in the *leisure* of our thoughts, or upon any *extraordinary* emergency.

1. Statedly in our *retirements* for the worship of God. When we *enter into our closet*, according to the command of our Lord, [Matt. vi. 6.] for those exercises of devotion in which the pleasure of a christian's life so much consists, and which contribute so much to his fitness for the service of God, in the place where providence has set him: when, I say, we retire to converse with heaven, can any thing be more proper than to reflect upon *the solemnities* we *lately* attended? and may it not be expected to put our spirits into a proper frame for the devotions upon which
we

we are entering? Confeſſion, humiliation, prayer, and praiſe, are the employments of the ſacred ſeaſon; the time we allot for ſecret worſhip and recollecting the view, which we had of Chriſt *at his table*, can hardly fail (by the bleſſing of GOD) to diſpoſe us for every part of the *cloſet*-ſervice. If we carry a *crucified* Jeſus in our minds, as we had him ſet before us at the ordinance; with what brokenneſs of heart, for inſtance, ſhall we confeſs and bewail thoſe tranſgreſſions for which he was *wounded*, and thoſe iniquities for which he was *bruiſed*? [Iſaiah liii. 5] When we look upon him whom *we have pierced*, ſhall we not be diſpoſed to *mourn as one mourneth for* his *only* ſon, *and be in bitterneſs for him, as one that is in bitterneſs for* his *firſt born?* [Zech. xii 10.] At the table of the Lord we ſee the *evil* of *ſin* repreſented in the ſtrongeſt colours, and in a manner moſt ſuited to affect: we ſee it as it were in its full triumph, delivering over the *bleſſed body* of the Son of GOD to wounds, torture, and death, and throwing ſuch a dreadful gloom over his *holy ſoul*, as would have eternally confounded an angel of light; for it made him, whom all the angels of God worſhip, cry out, *My* GOD, *my* GOD, *why haſt thou forſaken me?* And *generally* we are in a peculiar manner affected with what is there ſo

repre-

reprefented: our hearts being warmed beforehand by reading books of devotion, by clôfe meditation, abftraction from objects of fenfe, and matters of a lower nature, and efpecially by the influences of the Holy Spirit, given in anfwer to prayers made with more than ordinary frequency and fervour. Now it is known, that ftrong and deep impreffions, not only laft long, but are more eafily revived, when the mind exerts itfelf upon a proper occafion; this may be obferved in *common* cafes. what a fund of *joy* or *forrow* has that perfon at hand, who has had his mind wrought up into any great degree of fenfibility upon any *extraordinary* adventure? This obfervation may be applied to matters of a *fpiritual* nature, and will be an argument, why we fhould fet the fufferings of Chrift before us (as we have feen them reprefented in the fanctuary) in the reft of our exercifes of devotion, as well as in the acts of repentance and mortification: the life of prayer and praife is the acting of faith, hope, love, joy, and gratitude; and how the mind will be raifed into fuch fentiments by recollecting what we faw, felt, and tafted, when all thefe graces were in their higheft exercife upon the moft folemn occafion, I need not more particularly reprefent; I only advife to make the *experiment*, and let the *event* fpeak.

I fhall

I shall only observe farther, what use this may be of to *fix* a *wandering* mind   In some constitutions the imagination will have a scene, and can hardly be kept from roving, like the *fool's eye, to the ends of the earth:* [Prov. xvii. 24] this many know to the vexation of their souls: and how far its being possessed with the images of this great solemnity, as connected with the cross and throne of him *who was dead, and is alive, and lives and reigns for evermore,* may be of service in such a case, I only offer to consideration.

2 In the *leisure* of our thoughts, and *intervals* of business, it may also be very proper to turn our minds towards this *great solemnity* of our religion, and reflect upon what passed on that occasion; particularly, when we last remembered the author of it, shewed forth his death, professed our relation to him, and made our vows.   Whatever our stated business is, it must have intervals, and the mind, as well as body, must relax, and how pleasant soever it be, human nature generally requires diversion and amusement.   In this perhaps, earth differs from heaven; and if there are people of a different make, I have no concern with them, but only to congratulate their happiness. The generality of Christians will, I believe, acknowledge the case to be as I have represented it: and seeing the mind will be *al-*

ways

ways busy (though it cannot be *always intent*) may not some of its leisure thoughts be thus directed? I am not excluding a thousand innocent objects, which are not directly spiritual; but advising to give our thoughts about them a *religious cast* (may I call it?) or *spiritual tincture*, by throwing in something divine *en passant*, transiently, and in a secret manner not to be observed. And what *so proper* to this purpose, as the *idea* of him, who so lately entertained us at his table, and gave us his presence to make the *royal dainties* incomparably delicious? If any of us had been thus honoured by an earthly prince, it would possess our minds, and hang upon our imagination, perhaps more than a wise man would wish. If in the *present* case we were thus affected, would it not be with *good reason*, and might it not answer a *good end*? the frequent bearing our minds towards these objects, would *prevent* a great many *silly* thoughts, and *keep out a* great many *evil* ones; would help to poize and balance our minds, and preserve us from being overset with disagreeable occurrences, or carried away with unreasonable transports, when we meet with such as are more pleasing.

And as this *would be useful, it is* certainly *practicable.* There is nothing necessary to it, but that spiritual-mindedness, which is the beauty, strength, and even life of christianity;

ſtianity; as they very well know, who *fa-vour the things of God*, and have their *ſenſes exerciſed*, [Heb. v 14] who know what it is to have their *hearts where their treaſures are*; *to ſeek thoſe things which are above, where Chriſt ſitteth at the right hand of God*; to have *Chriſt dwell in their hearts by faith*; and their *converſation in heaven*, in oppoſition to thoſe *nominal profeſſors*, who only mind *earthly things* ſuch as underſtand what they read, *Yea doubtleſs, and I count all things but loſs, for the excellency of the knowledge of Chriſt Jeſus my Lord*. [Philip. iii. 8] The devout *Jews*, who were under a darker diſpenſation, which had only a *ſhadow of good things to come, and not the very image of the things,* [Heb x 1] knew what it was to lay up the words of God in their heart, and in their ſoul, to bind them as a *ſign upon their hand, and a frontlet between their eyes*, and what they were to teach their children, undoubtedly they thought of themſelves, when they *ſat in the houſe, and when they walked by the way, when they lay down, and when they roſe up*. [Deut. xi 18, 19] and ſurely, as we have greater *advantages*, we are under ſtronger *obligations* to this purpoſe: and when we read of their vehement affection for the tabernacles, courts, and altar of God; and how their hearts were in the ways which lead thither, which is expreſſed by their *ſouls longing and fainting, and their heart and*

flesh

flesh crying out, &c. it may lead us to consider, that as Christ exhibited in the *highest*
gospel-solemnity, challenges such a regard
from us, so it is a *forcible* thing to be
under the daily influence of the memorials of
that body and *blood of his*, which is incomparably more valuable than all *the service of
the temple*, as being *typified by* it, and the *end
of* it.

In short, *knowledge is easy to him that un-
derstandeth :* an experienced christian will
easily take in what I aim at ; and the matter
is not hard to explain to others, who understand the *nature of man*, though they may be
strangers to *vital religion*, and the power of
godliness. Suppose a man's heart vehemently set upon a worldly object, the thing
he loves will be continually bearing upon
his mind, and following him into business,
diversion and company, as well as soliciting
his thoughts in secrecy and retirement ;
and that without prejudicing his management of other affairs ; nay, on the contrary, will quicken his motions, and brighten
his conduct, in a manner, which his acquaintance may easily observe. I could give instances, and quote authors, to this purpose.
I shall only transcribe a passage out of a
writer, whose skill in philosophy, and acquaintance with human nature, I admire,
(though I can by no means acquiesce in his
account of christianity ;) his words are these :
‘ In

' In all which things (*viz.* innocent diver-
' tifements) we are not to forget GOD (in
' whom we both live and are moved, *Acts*
' XVII. 20) as not to have always fome
' fecret referve to him, and fenfe of his
' fear and prefence, which alfo frequently
' exerts itfelt in the midft of thefe things
' by fome fhort afpirations and breathings :
' and that this may neither feem ftrange
' nor troublefome, I fhall clear it by one
' manifeft inftance, anfwerable to the ex-
' perience of all men. It will not be de-
' nied, that men ought to be more in the
' love of GOD, than of any other thing.
' Now it is plain, that men that are taken
' with love, whether it be of women, or
' any other thing, if it hath taken a deep
' place in the heart, and poffefs the mind,
' it will be hard for the man fo in love, to
' drive out of his mind the perfon or thing
' fo loved ; yea, in his eating, drinking,
' or fleeping, his mind will always have a
' tendency that way ; and in bufinefs or
' recreations, however intent he may be,
' there will be but a very fhort time per-
' mitted to pafs, but the mind will let fome
' ejaculations forth towards its beloved,'
&c. [*Barclay's Apol.* Prop. XV. §. 9.]

I fhall only add, if *wicked* men allow
themfelves to repeat paft fins in their imagination ; and *worldly-minded* people give up

fo

so many of their thoughts to romantic schemes, and are so often calling back former times, and past occurrences, and herein act according to the *genius* and temper of a fleshly mind, it cannot be thought *improper* for those, who are *born of the spirit*, and have at the Lord's table *tasted and seen that he is gracious*, to admit, indulge, and frequently call up the remembrance of such solemnities, in which GOD was pleased to make his glorious grace pass before them. Christ's *flesh is meat indeed*, and *his blood is drink indeed*; and by a frequent remembrance how we fed on him at his table, (if we do it in a serious believing manner) our souls will have (in this, as it were, rumination) a great help to their growth in grace, and increasing *with all the increase of God*, Colos. ii. 19.

3. Upon any *extraordinary emergency*, it might be advisable to recollect the solemnities of a preceding communion.

If any sore *affliction* befals us, we may very properly think of *him*, whose death we lately shewed forth, what great things he suffered, and how meekly and patiently he *humbled himself, and became obedient unto death, even the death of the cross*; and that, though he was a son, yet he *learned obedience by the things which he suffered*; how, *for the joy that was set before him, he endured the cross and despised the shame*, &c. and that he has *left*

us

us an example, that we should follow his steps.
Let us remember, that he bears a sympathi-
sing mind, having himself suffered; and in
virtue of the sacrifice he offered on the cross,
he is our powerful *intercessor*, that we may
have timely help and proper supports, re-
membring, also, that this he promised at
the table, where he sealed *to us*, as well as
we *to him*; and by these thoughts encourage
our addresses to him, who as he is the
*Father of our Lord Jesus Christ, is the Father
of mercies, and the* God *of all comfort, and
comforteth his people in all their tribulation.*
[2 Cor i. 3, 4.]

If the *great adversary* assaults us, let us
look unto *Jesus*, whom we have seen *set
forth as crucified:* let us call to mind and
plead it with him, that he was *manifested to
destroy the works of the devil*, and that, *having
spoiled principalities and powers, he made a shew
of them openly, triumphing over them* on his
cross. [*Col.* ii. 15] Let us remember how,
when *Satan* desired to have *Peter*, that he
might *sift him as wheat*, he prayed for the
disciple, *that his faith might not fail*; and how
by a look his Saviour recovered him out of
the snare of the devil—and let us humbly urge,
that as Jesus is *the same yesterday, to-day, and
for ever*, and his grace and power never the
less for his being removed and exalted; so
he gave us encouragement at his table to
expect

expect his presence in the combat, and his assistance when most sore beset.

If we find *corruption* working; let us recollect the views we had of the evil of sin in the sufferings of our Lord, and remember, that *our old man is crucified with him, that the body of sin might be destroyed, and that henceforth we might not serve sin*, [Rom. vi. 6.] calling to mind that of the Apostle; *forasmuch then as Christ hath suffered for us in the flesh, arm yourselves likewise with the same mind. for he that hath suffered in the flesh, hath ceased from sin, that he no longer should live the rest of his time in the flesh, to the lusts of the flesh, but to the will of God.* [1 Pet. iv. 1, 2.] Let us consider, that *we are planted in the likeness of his death :* especially, let us have recourse to the representations and transactions, which passed at the ordinance, when that, which may be considered as *our iniquity*, gives us trouble. We must *look* to a crucified *Jesus*, if we would *lay aside the sin which easily besets us* · [Heb. xii. 1] and in short, whatever duty requires self-denial, will never be performed kindly and pleasantly, without *considering him*, [Ver. 3.] not only as having given us an *example* upon the cross ; but as having *sealed* at his table the *promise*, both of assistance and reward according to the gospel ; the promises whereof, or (which is

3   the

the fame thing) the bleffings of the new covenant, this ordinance *applies* and *feals*, as well as *reprefents*. It cannot be doubted, that a diftinct review of our covenant is proper, when we are to perform any part of duty, which requires application and refolution this is the moft likely method to raife in us fuch fentiments, as will quicken our motions, and invigorate our whole man, enlarge our hearts, and make us go on with pleafure in the duties of our holy calling, thus may we *mount up with wings as eagles, run and not be weary, walk and not faint* [Ifa. xl 31]

CHAP. V.

Reprefenting the Advantages, *which will arife from the practice, which has been recommended; particularly in relation to* fucceeding Opportunities, &c.

THE benefit of conducting ourfelves, as hath been directed, after our having received the communion, may be reprefented in a twofold view, as it refpects the *paft* opportunity, or as it is connected with the profpect of *future* ones I fhall wave the *firft*, as fufficiently declared in the former part of this difcourfe, and

confine

confine myfelf to the *latter*, of which I would fpeak moie particularly. And here let it be confidered,

1. Whilft chriftians manage in fuch a manner, as has been recommended, their *habitual* preparednefs for the holy folemnity cannot well be called in queftion. Serious minds are often folicited by many *doubts* and *fcruples* about thofe qualifications which are prefuppofed to their actual preparation; whether they are really *born again, partakers of a divine nature, paffed from death to life,* and have the *love of God*, which is the *root of the matter*, dwelling in them. They fufpect their fincerity, and queftion whether they have moie than a name to live, and a form of godlinefs without the power; and as this keeps many from *ever approaching* the holy table, fo it often gives a great deal of *trouble* to fuch, who dare not allow themfelves in the total neglect of a plain duty, and keeps them *many times* away, when they have otherwife no *reafonable* pretence for abfenting. Various methods of addrefs have been ufed with thefe unhappy perfons. The *former* (*viz.* thofe who abfolutely refufe to comply with the command of Chrift upon this allegation) I am not now concerned with but as to the *latter*, I may in geneial fay, that an improper conduct after the folemnity feems to be the fource and foundation of their perplexing fcruples,

and

and uneafy tormenting fears, and the frequent omiffions confequent upon them: under a confcioufnefs of not having lived as communicants ought, they are afraid to repeat their attendances · or, if they force themfelves to offer this facrifice, they do it in a manner very *improper*, and the iffue is ufually very *uncomfortable*.

But now thofe, who accuftom themfelves to recollection and reflection after their participation, in fome fuch manner as has been reprefented, can hardly fail of growing up into an *habitual affurance* of their intereft in the bleffings of the gofpel-covenant; and, unlefs in *extraordinary* cafes, will have little doubt of their being *washed*, that is, *fanctified* and *juftified, in the name of the Lord Jefus, and by the fpirit of our God* · [1 Cor vi 11] and this matter being once happily fettled, the grand difficulty is over, and the principal ftumbling-block removed

2. Such a conduct will exceedingly facilitate our *actual* preparation Thoughts of Chrift taking rife from the view we had of him at his table, being by daily reflection become familiar to our minds, we fhall not need long and laborious application to put ourfelves into a fit difpofition for the ordinance. What a man is daily, and upon a variety of incidents, thinking of, he will more eafily apply himfelf to in due form

F 2 upon

upon solemn occasions, as he, who is continually thinking of his friend, and has a desire of pleasing him habitually soliciting his mind, will be ready to visit or receive him without much warning, especially when a sincere love and cordial respect is the main thing expected, and outward pomp or ceremony is of little or no consideration. The preparation of the heart for this sacrament consists in a readiness to act faith, love, repentance, resolution, submission, &c. upon the representations there made of Christ, and particularly his love in dying for us: and if this bear upon our minds in *daily* returns, and the intervals of our thoughts, besides our having recourse to it upon *special* emergencies; how readily may we attend, without having any more to do, than to dismiss our worldly thoughts for that season, and recollect ourselves, so as to attend wholly to the matter before us? Whereas such as, having performed their devotions at the Lord's table, think no more of Christ's dying love, till they have publick warning to prepare for another communion, and, perhaps, don't apply in good earnest to their preparations, till a very near approach of the season, must have a great deal to do with their hearts to get them in order; and may expect to suffer under that hurry and perplexity, which is usual in ordinary affairs, when men have delayed till
they

they are straitened in time, and are not in
a condition to bear many unavoidable incidents of interruption and avocation.

Many persons, who *have time enough* for
their *preparatory* exercises, yet find it very
difficult to *manage* to advantage, this may
possibly arise in some for want of instruction;
but generally is owing to a carnal frame,
which makes self-employment in spiritual
things uncouth and irksome: but having
been accustomed to such meditations, we
shall set about the work with proper alacrity
and address, and may ordinarily expect to
be free from that confusion, perplexity, and
insensibility, which attends a mind not used
to such employments · as a man, who is
accustomed to any particular business, and
has his mind upon it in leisure intervals,
will be more easily in readiness for it, than
one who seldom and with reluctance sets
about it. Our *former* sins will be more
easily recollected, and proper impressions
more freely revive, (besides our being like
to have fewer *fresh* ones to create us trouble)
we shall more easily adjust the account we
have to make up, discern the evidences of
our sincerity, and put on all those orna-
ments which make up the wedding-attire:
as garments of *daily use* are more easily found
and put on than a habit which we *seldom*
use, and wear only upon necessity or special
occasions. In short, he whose whole life is

an

an improvement of the exhibition of a crucified Jesus, will easily get ready for this part of publick worship, when providence gives opportunity.

3 By this means we shall *attend* in a more *worthy* or acceptable manner Such a conduct, as has been recommended, will gradually spiritualize our frame, and consequently make us more fit for the sublimer parts of worship. we shall thus become more ready at the exercise of every grace, which the occasion calls for *Faith*, as it respects *unseen things* in general, and *the mediator* in particular, will be easily drawn forth by one, who is daily conversing with things above, and has a crucified and glorified Jesus, as it were *dwelling in his heart*. [Eph. iii. 17] nor will there be so much need of that quickening expostulation, *where is your faith?* [Luke viii 25] or that, *how is it that you have no faith?* [Mark iv 40] Making allowance for extraordinary occurrences, persons who have *their senses* thus *exercised*, will be able with great ease to raise their minds up to the throne of God, at whose right hand *he sits, who was dead, and is alive, and lives for evermore* As he, who looks daily at a distant object, will more easily discover it than a stranger, or one disused to remote prospects; and a steep ascent grows easy by a frequent use. so it is in the exercise of that grace, in
which

which the mind opens to diſtant proſpects, and aſcends in divine contemplations. When we are called upon in the ſolemnity, to do it *in remembrance of him*, how eaſy will it be to turn the eyes of our mind to an object, which has been daily familiar to us? this *is* agreeable to *reaſon* and *true philoſophy*, and confirmed by *experience*. for ' long and con- ' ſtant habits of fixing one thing on the ' imagination, begets a ready diſpoſition in ' the nerves to produce again the ſame ' image, till the thought of it becomes ' ſpontaneous and natural like breathing, ' or the motion of the heart, which the ' machine performs without the conſent of ' the will.' [Dr. *Cheyne's Eſſay on Long Life*, p. 156, 157.] ' And there is no doubt to be ' made, but the organs of ſenſation, and ' thoſe the mind uſes in its intellectual ' operations, may be likewiſe improved, ' ſtrengthened, and perfected by conſtant ' uſe and proper application,' as the ſame author obſerves [P 161.] to which conſi- deration we are taught from *ſcripture* to add (as a matter of the higheſt conſequence) the promiſe of GOD's grace, and the more plen- tiful effuſions of his ſpirit, which ſhall be given to thoſe who improve their talents ; *to him that hath, it ſhall be given.* The ſame may be ſaid of *repentance*, and *love* in all the expreſſions of it, and every thing which is the proper employment of the ſacred

F 4   hour.

hour If the heart be kept warm by *habitual* applications to its great object, it will be more ready to flame out on *solemn occasions*, in those ardent defires after GOD, without which all our bodily exercife will be of no advantage to ourfelves, and not at all pleafing or acceptable to him, whom we profefs to ferve —And can there be a better method to keep it fo, than that which I have propofed?

There will be alfo this advantage arifing from what I have offered; that we fhall not be fo apt to have our mind *diftracted* with the *variety of fervice*, which we are called to at the ordinance. We are there to make various reflections, and exprefs a great diverfity of refentments, love to GOD, hatred of fin, felf-loathing, and deep humiliation, hope, joy, fubmiffion, refolution, thankfgiving, &c This *multiplicity* of addrefs is apt to puzzle and confound fuch, as are unpractifed and unaccuftomed to fpiritual and devotional exercifes, they are in danger of having their minds perplexed, their thoughts fhattered, and their hearts funk with fear of not attending duly to every thing, which the cafe requires. Whereas, in the practice of what I have recommended, we fhall find this benefit, that our transitions from one thing to another will be lefs difficult, and our minds will be more eafily conducted from one fcene to another, as they

fhall

shall open to us; or, if any thing be omitted, a consciousness of what has passed in the exercise of recollection will comfort us, and especially a prospect of calling every thing over more particularly in the following opportunities of review

One thing more may be worthy our consideration, that by the method proposed we are like to be more fit for the *proper* service of the occasion, which is holy *rejoicing* and thanksgiving. The sacrament of the Lord's Supper is a *festival* solemnity, in it we should *serve the Lord with gladness, and come before his presence with singing, enter into his gates with thanksgiving, and into his courts with praise, be thankful unto him, and bless his name* [Psal. c. 2, 4] Now *this* no man is so well qualified for, as he who retains upon his mind the favour and relish of former sacramental transactions, and has kept up their influence upon his heart and ways, by such stated and occasional recollections as have been recommended. Such are likely to possess the soul in a steady chearfulness and serenity, and have most reason to expect those peculiar elevations and enlargements which GOD sometimes indulges, not only as a reward of their diligence and spirituality, but as a support under future trials and sore dispensations: however, their *soul will magnify the Lord, and their spirit rejoice in God their Saviour*. [Luke 1 46, 47.] and, unless

F 5   some-

fomething *extraordinary* occur, their *foul will be fatisfied as with marrow and fatnefs, and their mouth praife God with joyful lips*. [Pfal. lxiii. 5.] when they *look on him whom they have pierced, and mourn*, even this mourning will be confiftent with, yea, friendly to the *rejoicing in Chrift Jefus*. In a word, fuch perfons are likely, in the remembrance of an unfeen Jefus, to *rejoice with joy unfpeakable, and full of glory*, [1 Pet. i 8] and may expect to return from the ordinance, with a fettled peace and ferenity of mind, which will fit them for the duties of their *general* and *particular* calling; and to experience what is fignified in that expreffion, *the joy of the Lord is their ftrength*. [Nch viii 10.] And then continuing in their ufual courfe of recollecting and improving what has paffed at the ordinance, for maintaining and increafing a fpiritual frame and heavenly converfation, they will have abundant evidence that they did not ' cheat themfelves with their ' own fancies, inftead of a fenfe of GOD's ' love; like thofe who, walking in the va- ' nities and ways of this world, yet boaft of ' their fenfe of the love of GOD.' [Dr. *Owen of Temptation*, p. 119.]

Thus I have reprefented the advantages which will arife from the due improvement of *one* communion, in reference to fuch as we fhall *afterwards* have the opportunity of attending upon. What farther I have to

offer

offer in recommendation of the practice, shall be under three heads.

1. By this means we shall not be tempted to think much of *frequent* communion. We are told the *primitive christians* communicated every day; to be sure they did every Lord's day; it was a part of their stated worship. I shall not pretend to find fault with the custom of *protestant* churches; but I hope I may say without offence, that the reason why the primitive practice has received so great an alteration, appears to be founded in one of these two things: either *a degree of superstition*, in setting this ordinance in a higher preference to other sacred appointments, than I can find any warrant for in *scripture*, or else *a want of* that *spiritual-mindedness*, or being in good earnest in matters of religion, which was once the glory of the churches of Christ. and perhaps, a mixture of *both*. However, may I not say, if a right improvement of the communion was made in some such manner as I have been recommending, we should not be so forward in making excuses, when providence offers an opportunity? how often are people's places empty, when they are not hindered by any just occasion? which would not be, if they had maintained that spiritual frame in any good measure, into which their converse with a *crucified Redeemer* brought them.

F 6. We

We let down our watch, and go off our guard, give our hearts a loofe to folly and vanity, or plunge too deep into worldly amufements : this makes it difficult to re-collect ourfelves, and difpofes us to invent reafons for our omiffion , and one neglect makes way for another, till *at laft* 'tis well if we do not wholly eftrange ourfelves from attendance on Chrift at his table.——And the confequence of this is often very tremen-dous ; firft a carelefs life, and then an ad-miffion of fuch principles as may ferve to fupport it , all which would be happily pre-vented by the method I have been pro-pofing.

2. Another good effect of this conduct would be, that we fhall not be fo much dejected, if we are *necessarily put by* our ufual and ftated attendance. Whilft I reprove needlefs omiffions, I own there may be real occafions for abfenting ourfelves from this ordinance not only bodily indifpofitions, travelling in foreign countries, the abfence of proper perfons to adminifter it, but fome circumftances befides, of which others may not be fo proper judges as ourfelves : this indeed, when it happens, is an *affliction*, and may be refented as fuch ; but we ought not to fpoil the peace of our mind upon this account. The *habitual* fpirituality of our frame, which refults from the review of what we have experienced of the prefence of GOD

at

at his table, will be a great means to com-
pofe us, and prevent any excefs of uneafi-
nefs, which might elfe arife in fuch a cafe:
let fuch as are kept from a *frefh* oppoi tu-
nity, recollect what paffed at *the laft*, and
it may, by the bleffing of G o d, anfwer
the fame end as their renewed attendance
would do. Thus a man may as it were
communicate by himfelf; and, though *abfent
in body, be prefent in fpirit*, with the churches
of Chrift and this will be more eafy to
thofe, who have accuftomed themfelves to
the review which has been recommended.
But always remember, it muft be a *real ne-
ceffity*, and not *a pretence* of our own, othei-
wife we are guilty of the neglect of a plain
duty, and no *fuccedareum* oi equivalent fhall
be admitted in its room

3 This will alfo afford comfort, if thro'
bodily indifpofition, or extraordinary acci-
dents, we fhould *not find ourfelves in fuch a
frame as was expected, or has been ufual.* They
who fcarce think of the facrament, but
when the time of the folemnity is juft at
hand, and then do not find what they propofed, are apt to fuffer under the ill effects
of their difappointment, either they are
inconfolable, or, which is worfe, grow *in-
different* about the matter. But fuch as make
it their bufinefs, in the interval of facraments,
to recollect and improve the *laft*, will have
a relief againft both thefe evils; efpecially

in.

in the confcioufnefs of their fincerity, and that
their miffing of what they aimed at, has not
proceeded from a flothful, worldly, or otherwife carnal mind ; and fo, inftead of terrifying
themfelves with the fad thought of having *eat
and drank damnation* to themfelves, they will
fubmit to it, as they do to other unavoidable
affliction., and confider it like them, im-
proveable to the purpofes of humility and
felf-abafement, and t . in the mere mercy
of a gracious God, through a prevailing Mediator. But then we muft fee to it, that we
do not encourage ourfelves in floth and indif-
ference by that, which was never defigned for
that end.

Many more advantages arifing from the
due improvement *of,* and walking regularly
after the participation of this great ordinance
of our religion, might be reprefented with
eafe · but the end I propofed, being anfwered
as far as lies in my power, I fhall conclude,
and recommend the attempt to the divine
benediction.

APPEN-

APPENDIX.

The following Prayers are borrowed from the late excellent and reverend Mr. Matthew Henry *.

I. *A Prayer for a* particular *Perſon*, before *receiving of the ſacrament of the* Lord's Supper.

MOST holy, and bleſſed, and gracious Lord God, with all humility and reverence, I here preſent myſelf before thee, to ſeek thy face, and intreat thy favour, and as an evidence of thy good will towards me, to beg that I may experience thy good work in me

I acknowledge myſelf unworthy, utterly unworthy of the honour; unfit, utterly unfit for the ſervice to which I am now called. It is an ineſtimable privilege, that I am admitted ſo often to hear from thee in thy word, and to ſpeak to thee in prayer; and yet, as if this had been a ſmall matter, I am now invited into communion with thee at thy holy table, there to celebrate the memorial of my Saviour's death, and to partake by faith of the precious benefits which flow from it. I, who deſerve not the crumbs, am called to eat of the children's bread.

* *Vid.* His *Method of Prayer,* &c. at the end.

O Lord, I thank thee for the inſtitution of this bleſſed ordinance, this precious legacy and token of love which the Lord Jeſus left to his church; that it is preſerved to this age; that it is adminiſtred in this land; that I am admitted to it, and have now before me an opportunity to partake of it· Lord, grant that I may not receive thy grace here in vain.

O thou, who haſt called me to the marriage ſupper of the Lamb, give me the wedding-garment, work in me a diſpoſition of ſoul, and all thoſe pious and devout affections which are ſuited to the ſolemnities of this ordinance, and requiſite to qualify me for an acceptable and advantageous participation of it. Behold the fire and the wood, all things are now ready; but where is the lamb for the burnt offering? Lord, provide thyſelf a lamb, by working in me all that, which thou requireſt of me upon this occaſion The preparation of the heart, and the anſwer of the tongue, are both from thee; Lord, prepare my unprepared heart for communion with thee.

Lord, I confeſs I have ſinned againſt thee, I have done fooliſhly, very fooliſhly, for fooliſhneſs is bound up in my heart; I have ſinned, and have come ſhort of the glory of God, I have come ſhort of glorifying thee, and deſerve to come ſhort of being glorified with thee. The imagination of my heart is evil continually, and the bias of my corrupt nature is very ſtrong towards the world, and the

the flesh, and the gratifications of sense; but towards God, and Christ, and Heaven, I move slowly, and with a great many stops and pauses. Nay, there is in my carnal mind a wretched aversion to divine and spiritual things. I have misspent my time, trifled away my opportunities, have followed after lying vanities, and forsaken my own mercies. God be merciful to me a sinner! for how little have I done since I came into the world of the great work, that I was sent into the world about!

Thou hast taken me into covenant with thee, for I am a baptized christian, set apart for thee, and sealed to be thine; thou hast laid me, and I also have laid myself, under all possible obligations to love thee, and serve thee, and live to thee. But I have started aside from thee like a deceitful bow: I have not made good my covenant with thee, nor hath the temper of my mind, and the tenor of my conversation, been agreeable to that holy religion which I make profession of, to my expectations from thee, and engagements to thee. I am bent to backslide from the living God; and if I were under the law, I were undone; but I am under grace, a covenant of grace, which leaves room for repentance, and promiseth pardon upon repentance, which invites even backsliding children to return, and promiseth that their backslidings shall be healed. Lord, I take hold of this covenant, seal it to me at

thy

thy table. There let me find my heart truly humbled for fin, and forrowing for it after a godly fort. O that I may there look on him whom I have pierced, and mourn, and be in bitterneſs for him; that there I may fow in tears, and receive a broken Chriſt into a broken heart. and there let the blood of Chriſt, which ſpeaks better things than that of *Abel*, be ſprinkled upon my conſcience, to purify and pacify that there let me be aſſured that thou art reconciled to me, that mine iniquities are pardoned, and that I ſhall not come into condemnation. There ſay unto me, Be of good chear, thy ſins are forgiven thee.

And that I may not come unworthily to this bleſſed ordinance, I beſeech thee, lead me into a more intimate and experimental acquaintance with Jeſus Chriſt, and him crucified; with Jeſus Chriſt, and him glorified; that knowing him, and the power of his reſurrection, and the fellowſhip of his ſufferings, and being by his grace planted in the likeneſs of both, I may both diſcern the Lord's body, and ſhew forth the Lord's death.

Lord, I deſire by a true and lively faith to cloſe with Jeſus Chriſt, and conſent to him as my Lord, and my GOD, I here give up myſelf to him as my prophet, prieſt and king, to be ruled, and taught, and ſaved by him; this is my beloved, and this is my friend. None but Chriſt, none but Chriſt. Lord, increaſe this faith in me, perfect what is lacking in it; and enable me, in receiving the
bread.

bread and wine at thy table by a lively faith, to receive Christ Jesus the Lord. O let the great gospel doctrine of Christ's dying to save sinners, which is represented in that ordinance, be meat and drink to my soul, meat indeed, and drink indeed, let it be both nourishing and refreshing to me, let it be both my strength and my song, and be the spring both of my holiness and of my comfort. And let such deep impressions be made upon my soul, by the actual commemoration of it, as may abide always upon me, and have a powerful influence upon me in my whole conversation, that the life I now live in the flesh I may live by the faith of the son of God, who loved me, and gave himself for me.

Lord, I beseech thee fix my thoughts; let my heart be engaged to approach unto thee, that I may attend upon thee without distraction. Draw out my desires towards thee, give me to hunger and thirst after righteousness, that I may be filled; and to draw near to thee with a true heart, and in full assurance of faith, and since I am not straitened in thee, O let me not be straitened in my own bosom.

Draw me, Lord, and I will run after thee: O send out thy light and thy truth, let them lead and guide me, pour thy Spirit upon me, put thy Spirit within me, to work in me both to will and to do that which is good; and leave me not to myself. Awake, O north wind, and come thou south, and blow upon

my

my garden; come, O bleſſed Spirit of grace, and enlighten my mind with the knowledge of Chriſt, bow my will to the will of Chriſt, fill my heart with the love of Chriſt, and confirm my reſolutions to live and die with him.

Work in me (I pray thee) a principle of holy love and charity towards all men, that I may forgive my enemies, (which by thy grace I heartily do) and may keep up a ſpiritual communion in faith, hope, and holy love, with all that in every place call on the name of Jeſus Chriſt our Lord. Lord, bleſs them all, and particularly that congregation with which I am to join in this ſolemn ordinance. Good Lord, pardon every one that engageth his heart to ſeek God, the Lord God of his fathers, though not cleanſed according to the purification of the ſanctuary. Hear my prayers, and heal the people.

Lord, meet me with a bleſſing, a Father's bleſſing at thy table; grace thine own inſtitutions with thy preſence, and fulfil in me all the good pleaſure of thy goodneſs, and the work of faith with power, for the ſake of Jeſus Chriſt my bleſſed Saviour and Redeemer, to him, with the Father, and the Eternal Spirit, be everlaſting praiſes. *Amen.*

II. *A prayer,* after *receiving of the* Lord's Supper.

O Lord, my God and my Father in Jeſus Chriſt, I can never ſufficiently admire the condeſcenſion of thy grace to me; what

is man that thou doſt thus magnify him, and
the ſon of man that thou viſiteſt him ! Who
am I ? And what is my houſe, that thou haſt
brought me hitherto, haſt brought me into
thy banqueting-houſe, and thy banner over
me hath been love ? I have reaſon to ſay, that
a day in thy courts, an hour at thy table, is
better, far better, than a thouſand days, than
ten thouſand hours elſewhere, it is good for
me to draw near to God. Bleſſed be God for
the privileges of his houſe, and thoſe com-
forts with which ne makes his people joyful
in his houſe of prayer.

But I have reaſon to bluſh and be aſhamed
of myſelf, that I have not been more affected
with the great things, which have been ſet
before me, and offered to me at the Lord's
table O what a vain, fooliſh, trifling heart
have I ! when I would do good, even then
evil is preſent with me ; good Lord, be merciful to me, and pardon the iniquity of my
holy things, and let not my manifold defects
in my attendance upon thee be laid to my
charge, or hinder my profiting by the ordinance.

I have now been commemorating the death
of Chriſt : Lord, grant that, by the power of
that, ſin may be crucified in me, the world
crucified to me, and I to the world, and
enable me ſo to bear about with me continually the dying of the Lord Jeſus, as that the
life alſo of Jeſus may be manifeſted in my
mortal body.

I have

I have now been receiving the precious benefits, which flow from Chrift's death: Lord, grant that I may never lofe, may never forfeit thofe benefits; but, as I have received Chrift Jefus the Lord, give me grace fo to walk in him, and to live as one that am not my own, but am bought with a price, glorifying God with my body and fpirit, which are his.

I have now been renewing my covenant with thee, and engaging myfelf afrefh to thee to be thine; now, Lord, give me grace to perform my vow Keep it always in the imagination of the thought of my heart, and eftablifh my way before thee. Lord, prefeve me by thy grace, that I may never return again to folly: after God hath fpoken peace, may I never, by my loofe and carelefs walking, undo what I have been doing to-day: but, having my heart enlarged with the confolations of God, give me to run the way of thy commandments with chearfulnefs and conftancy, and ftill to hold faft my integrity.

This precious foul of mine, which is the work of thine own hands, and the purchafe of thy Son's blood, I commit into thy hands, to be fanctified by thy Spirit and grace, and wrought up into a conformity to thy holy will in every thing Lord, fet up thy throne in my heart, write thy law there, fhed abroad thy love there, and bring every thought within me into obedience to thee, to the commanding power of thy law, and the constraining power of thy love. Keep through thine own name that which I commit unto thee, keep it against that day when it shall be called for, let me be preserved blameless to the coming of thy glory, that I may then be presented faultless with exceeding joy.

All my outward affairs I submit to the disposal of thy wise and gracious Providence; Lord, save my soul, and then, as to other things, do what thou pleasest with me, only make all Providences to work together for my spiritual and eternal advantage. Let all things be pure to me, and give me to taste covenant love in common mercies; and by thy grace, let me be taught both how to want, and how to abound, how to enjoy prosperity, and how to bear adversity, as becomes a christian; and at all times let thy grace be sufficient for me, and mighty in me, to work in me both to will and to do that which is good of thine own good pleasure.

And that in every thing I may do my duty, and stand complete in it, let my heart be enlarged in love to Jesus Christ, and affected with the height and depth, the length and breadth of that love of his to me, which passeth all conception and expression.

And as an evidence of that love, let my mouth be filled with his praises: worthy is the Lamb that was slain, to receive blessing and honour, and glory and power, for he

was

was flain, and hath redeemed a chofen rem-
nant unto GOD by his blood, and made
them to him kings and priefts. Blefs the
Lord, O my foul, and let all that is within
me blefs his holy name, who forgiveth all
mine iniquities, and healeth all my difeafes ;
who redeemeth my life from deftruction,
and crowneth me with loving kindnefs and
tender mercy ; who having begun a good
work, will perform it unto the day of Chrift.
As long as I live I will blefs the Lord, I will
praife my GOD while I have any being ; and
when I have no being on earth, I hope to
have a being in heaven, to be doing it better.
O let me be borne up in everlafting arms, and
carried from ftrength to ftrength, till I appear before GOD in *Zion* ; for Jefus fake, who
died for me, and rofe again, in whom I defire
to be found living and dying. Now to GOD
the Father, Son, and Spirit, be afcribed
kingdom, power and glory, henceforth and
for ever. *Amen.*

F I N I S.

Lightning Source UK Ltd.
Milton Keynes UK
UKHW031450070219
336895UK00005B/140/P